# THE WOUNDED

&

## GRACE ABOUNDING

*Other titles in the Wounded Pilgrim series*
*edited by Brian Thorne*

## THE DARK UNCERTAINTY
David and Sarah Clark

## WRESTLING WITH FAMILY LIFE
Susan Walrond-Skinner

# GRACE ABOUNDING

## WRESTLING WITH SIN
## AND GUILT

Dorin Barter

*Where sin abounded, grace did much more abound.*
ROMANS 5:20

DARTON · LONGMAN + TODD

First published in 1993 by
Darton Longman & Todd Ltd
1 Spencer Court
140–142 Wandsworth High Street
London SW18 4JJ

© 1993 Dorin Barter

ISBN 0-232-51975-7

A catalogue record for this book is available
from the British Library

Phototypeset in 10½/13pt Bembo by Intype, London
Printed and bound in Great Britain
at the University Press, Cambridge

This book
is my acknowledgement
of all that I have learned
from
P. F. J.

*4 August 1991*

## CONTENTS

|  | | |
|---|---|---|
| | *Foreword* by Brian Thorne | ix |
| | *Preface* | xi |
| | *Acknowledgements* | xiii |
| | Prologue: Pilgrims and Explorers | 1 |
| 1. | Sin and Guilt – and Choice | 7 |
| 2. | Two Ethics | 32 |
| 3. | The Womb of the Spirit | 52 |
| 4. | Masks, Knots and Bruises | 71 |
| 5. | Paradoxical Wounds | 85 |
| 6. | A Blow to the Heart | 99 |
| 7. | Letting Go and Losing | 122 |
| 8. | There is No Wrath in God | 145 |
| 9. | The Pain of God | 164 |
| | Epilogue: Traveller's Harvest | 188 |
| | *Further Reading* | 194 |
| | *Notes* | 197 |

# FOREWORD

The 'Wounded Pilgrim' series is inspired by the belief that spiritual growth demands an openness to experience and a willingness to accept the challenge of self-knowledge despite the suffering, confusion and agony of spirit which this can involve.

In different ways each book attempts to focus on the brokenness of the spiritual pilgrim and to face those areas of pain and struggle which are all too frequently swept under the carpet by the institutional churches or to which simplistic or dogmatic answers are given. The hope is that such books, written by those who do not flinch from the exploration of personal suffering and who acknowledge the complexity of social and psychological reality, will touch the hearts and minds of those who yearn for nourishment on their spiritual pilgrimage but who find the life of the Churches hard to bear, or who have long since abandoned the practice of institutional religion. The series is also a passionate response to the Churches' call for a decade of evangelism or evangelization. It reflects, however, a deep antipathy to the spirit of crusading and triumphalism and to the tone of theological and moral certitude which not infrequently characterize evangelistic campaigns.

The authors in this series write from the perspective of those who have no glib answers. They share a common determinatiion to be true to themselves and to the reality which they experience. In short, they are courageous seekers who write in the hope that their own honesty will offer strength and a sense of companionship to those who have perhaps been deeply hurt by life's events and not least by the judgementalism of what sometimes passes for spiritual guidance.

BRIAN THORNE

# PREFACE

It is usually necessary, nowadays, to say something about the use of personal pronouns, both for God and for people.

I use 'he' for God. Writing about some subjects, I might use 'it' and would then be referring to the Godhead, and not to the God with whom I feel in relationship. For me, the word 'she' is not appropriate, but I know and understand that other people would find it more suitable.

The way in which I experience God not only determines which pronoun I prefer to use, but also underlies everything that I have written in this book; and in case the masculine pronoun suggests to my readers certain beliefs and attitudes which are not mine, I want to say a little about my theology.

I believe in God who is incarnate in the whole material universe and is transcendent utterly beyond my understanding. God is ALL, and what he (or it) is *more* than ALL that is, he knows, not I; but that God *is* ALL and more than ALL I am certain. The very core of 'God', which paradoxically is also the full extent of God, is, I know, immeasurably more than the Divine Person I can relate to – it is the Godhead, the Limitless about which we can say nothing, the Coherency. It is the I AM, and we limited humans cannot know it in itself. But since I as a person can reach out to God and experience the contact which results as a personal relationship, I can reasonably conclude that he too (among all else which he, or she, or it is, beyond my conceiving) is also a person.

The personal God in *my* life is masculine, is Lord and co-worker – which only says how I relate, and does not describe at all the innumerable ways in which he-and-she can and does relate to others. For me this relationship is one of love, in that it both causes and enables me to love, and I experience it as the receiving of love. For me, personally, God is Love.

The Godhead, the Limitless En-Sof of the Kabbalists which is 'total unity beyond comprehension', is, I believe – and here I do have to come into belief, not experience – also Love; is Relationship. The eternal energy of the Godhead fills all the spaces between the objects of the universe, just as it fills all those objects with their life. It is this energy of Love which holds them in·relationship, experienced as gravity between planets, electromagnetism between atoms, compassionate bonds between people. The energy which forms and maintains relationships is Love, and the energy which formed and maintains that total relationship which we call the universe is the creative and sustaining Love of God. All relating is the Godhead and God working. All wrestling with sin and guilt is God working within us and us working with God to express the relationship which we have with him.

Pronouns for people are a much simpler matter. I find 'humankind' to be a simple and acceptable synonym for 'man' or 'mankind'; and 'he and she' can often be used instead of just 'he'. But not always; it becomes clumsy and unrhythmic when repeated too often. 'S/he' I find impossible. Using 'she' and 'he' in alternate paragraphs or chapters is jolting, and can blur the distinction we sometimes do want to make between men and women; and the English language has almost lost the use of the anonymous, inclusive 'one'. So sometimes I say only 'he'; it is then a purely aesthetic choice which I hope you, the reader, can accept.

DORIN BARTER

# ACKNOWLEDGEMENTS

Warm thanks are due to my son Chris for very sharp examination of some chapters. I have benefited from the clear analysis which he brings to all arguments, and am especially grateful that he applied this skill to unfamiliar subject matter. The Julian Study Group provided valuable early input, and continued to show interest and give encouragement; the support of Joy Croft has been especially welcome. I am glad to have had preliminary readings of the whole manuscript by Michael Mitlehner, who criticized but respected my theology, and by Salvo Mitale and Laurence Lucas, who both served as the sort of readers (and friends) I hope to be addressing.

I am also indebted to my editor, Brian Thorne – for living so close, for being so sensitive, for taking a chance on me in the very first place. His suggestions have always been thoughtful and helpful.

Jill Hall, dear friend, knows and cares just how much heartache some parts of this book cost me; and she knows how grateful I am.

I didn't know I was a pilgrim –
no-one had come to tell –
I'd passed no miracles on foot
there was no warning bell.
I heard no prayer, no dead man spoke,
I passed no sacred sign:
I didn't know I was a pilgrim
until I touched the shrine.

MARGIAD EVANS, *A Ray of Darkness*
(John Calder 1978), p. 176

A person may travel through labyrinthine paths to reach the land of wholeness.

CHRISTOPHER BRYANT, *The Heart in Pilgrimage*
(DLT 1980), p. 31

'We know our God from His energies,' wrote Saint Basil, 'but we do not claim that we can draw near to His essence. For His energies come down to us, but His essence remains unapproachable.' . . . These energies . . . are God Himself in His action and revelation to the world . . . In relation to man, the divine energy is in fact nothing less than the *grace of God*; grace is not just a 'gift' of God, not just an object which God bestows on men, but a direct manifestation of the living God Himself, a personal confrontation between creature and Creator.

TIMOTHY WARE, *The Orthodox Church*
(Penguin 1963), pp. 77–8

Into this climate of theological cheerlessness and doom Julian's message burst like a joyous song . . . His graciousness, she pleaded, could be counted upon on all the occasions of life, and not least in our 'failing' and 'falling' and 'dying', for here too 'the sweet eye of pity is never turned away from us, and the operation of mercy does not cease' . . . what at least is certain is that we can never fall outside God's love. Our falling, Julian might well have said, is not so much a falling into sin as a falling into the arms of God's mercy.

ROBERT LLEWELYN, *With Pity not With Blame*<br>(DLT 1982), pp. 21–2

# PROLOGUE: PILGRIMS AND EXPLORERS

This is a book about grace, more than about sin and guilt; it is about weakness and failure more than badness and disobedience.

Of course it is true that we all need to examine guilt and to repudiate sin, and we are required to make good the harm we have caused. But although we have to make our own efforts, we are always aided by gifts of grace. Discernment enables us to see into our guilt clearly and to assess its source; realistic self-knowledge helps us to name our sin truthfully; and the most effective gift of all is a hunger for the loving God who draws us out of that darkness and confusion. We are never left friendless in sin; but saving grace comes in difficult guises, and in the end what matters most is our willingness to accept it whatever its form.

The times when we clearly feel the support of grace are like reaching harbour after a storm. We come upon such refuges, sometimes too briefly but always with gladness, after the dark and fearful stages of our journeys, and we drop our anchor there in the hope of rest. The seaport names of my Newfoundland childhood are music to me: Seldom-Come-By and Come-By-Chance, Heart's Content, Bonne Bay and Heart's Delight, and, sweetest of all, Harbour Grace, safe landfall after the long Atlantic journey, named in thanksgiving and relief. I have said them like a litany sometimes, when the travelling was at its worst, seeing in my mind the small clear channels past the cliffs and dangerous rocks. The harbour of grace is the landfall of the pilgrim, sometimes only a short relief from the storms of sin and guilt, sometimes a full refuge at last, that part of the journey ended. Every time we go as far as we can towards where we believe we ought to be, and give up all our need for defined security and accept wherever it is that we have reached, then where we are *is* Harbour Grace.

But grace is also the ocean on which we have been travelling, through all the storms, and is not just the anchorage where we at last find rest. If we trust ourselves to that sea of grace, responding to it and using it, however the sinews of our vessels strain against the effort and fear, we can be sure that we are truly journeying. We will discover that the journey on and in grace is what we are here for; and that there is no essential difference between the ocean and its harbours. Indeed, we will learn that *everywhere* we travel is encompassed by grace. Its constancy upholds us in long desert dryness which tests our endurance, and its shelters are scattered throughout the mountains of fear and conflict to offer peace for a while between dangers. Grace offers us the journey itself, dark and unwelcome though it seems at first, for it brings us to a sweeter land than we could have found by our own searching.

Both pilgrims and explorers undertake such hazardous endeavours, crossing sea and land to reach far places, but the journeys prove to be different. A pilgrim is going to a particular shrine, more or less by an accepted route. The pilgrims to Canterbury or Compostella started out with a map, if only an oral one culled from the tales of other, returned travellers and from knowledgeable authorities who told them where to go and how to get there. Their dual motives were the devotion to God and reverence for holy places which first called them out, and the task of purgation which their effort would accomplish. By this old-fashioned word I mean cleansing oneself of whatever sins hinder one's devotion and eventual slow conformity to ideals of goodness and faith. On the whole, pilgrims knew what sort of people they wanted to be – or at least they were told clearly what sort they ought to be; and indeed, their social and ecclesiastical setting often gave them little choice.

It is not so different for the pilgrimage through sin and guilt. The map is the mores of society, codified in the law, and the doctrines of the church, and the standards of the community. The pilgrim follows the road which these describe, using them as best he or she may on strange and puzzling stretches of the route, reaching the shrine at last and discovering whether or not he can worship there – for the life which a conventional pilgrimage presupposes may turn out after all not to be possible, or even desirable, once it is clearly seen.

But nowadays many of us find ourselves on a pilgrimage to an unknown destination, no longer able to follow the old and familiar pointers or to accept the established maps. 'God is an undiscovered country',[1] and our way to him turns out, instead, to be an exploration. This too is a purging, but its end is to become one's real self, stripped of roles and familiar forms, creating a new and less secure life. Pilgrimage does not seem to have been a biblical concept, and there are only half a dozen references in my concordance; of these, one heart-aching quotation seems rather to be describing an exploration: 'These all died in the faith, not having received the promises, but having seen them afar off, and were persuaded of them, and embraced them, and confessed that they were strangers and pilgrims on the earth.'[2] Travelling through the strange lands of our lives, many of us find a new and unknown holy place, and worship there, hoping that others will join us so that we can make a new community. Having left those settled places which so often proved unsatisfactory for us, we cannot with integrity set out for the old shrines which no longer call to us. New pilgrims, having found the collective mores inadequate, must live by a new, personal response to sin and guilt in their lives. They become explorers.

Whether exploration or pilgrimage, this is a journey from and through darkness towards the light. Both our sin and our guilt seem darkness indeed, and our struggle with them shadows our lives and distorts everything we look at. If we are to travel through them, we must experience this darkness consciously, put it into words and images, and separate ourselves from it to some extent so that we can look at it in a different way. We have to be able to realize that sin and guilt are not all of nor even a major part of ourselves, that we can stand within our central selves and look at the darkness and be able to say, 'How dark it is; but *I* am not dark, I am someone who is looking at the darkness. So – what else could I look for, instead?' Then from that vantage point we begin to find signs of God even in the darkness, can find him in love and relationship, can perceive forgiveness, and search for a true way forward.

Sometimes we do not even know that we are, or will become, pilgrims; certainly we cannot predict whether we will become explorers. We may be wrestling so painfully with sin and guilt today, here in this particular place, that we never look up to notice what has changed, whether we are in fact getting somewhere as we struggle. But the pilgrim's perspective, or the explorer's, is one we need to develop, for to a great extent our endurance and persistence depend upon it. When we are burdened and hindered and sometimes cannot even believe in, much less glimpse, a goal, we are likely to despair and give up. We need the assurance that others have made similar efforts and have won through, that there is a pattern to our experiences and a route through them, and that the effort is supremely worthwhile.

However solitary my own journey has seemed externally, I have never been entirely alone. I have had so many true friends in books: Paul Tillich and Teilhard de Chardin, both encouraging guides when effort has narrowed perspective; Julian of Norwich, a neighbour I always appreciate though we may often disagree; the chance-met acquaintance, Frank Lake, who became my mentor for a decade; infuriating, inspiring Charles Williams; Christopher Bryant with his breadth of experience, and Alan Jones, whose way seems parallel to my own – they are fellow travellers, map-makers, companions. They are with us throughout all the following chapters, as though in conversations at wayside inns.

I hope that you and I will travel together, in this book. At the beginning of this journey, for all of us, there must first be experiences of the darkness of sin and woundedness, which I

## PROLOGUE

want to share with you as another pilgrim, one who has become an explorer. Together we will try to bring that fearful darkness out of its confusion and obscurity, to look at it with courage, and recognize it as part of our humanness, something we all have in common. Those difficult stages in which we face and admit our rebellion, isolation and brokenness have to be lived and felt fully. But when we clearly know and have admitted our condition, we can learn how to make our struggle with sin and guilt more effective, and can gain a sure hold on the reasons for making it, so that we will be encouraged to persevere. Then we will be able to move on into the release, the potential and the responsibility which we share with each other, and to travel into the light and the love of God, of self and neighbour.

# 1

# SIN AND GUILT – AND CHOICE

**It all depends on what you mean by—**

Words have so many meanings, to say nothing of their undertones and overtones, that all the 'big' words of our subject mean something different in every discussion and to every reader. Over the years, I have worked out my personal definitions for the words I will use in this book, especially 'sin', partly because I am the sort of person who prefers clarity, and partly to avoid real misunderstandings by trying to agree – first of all and foremost – on experiences and feelings, and then on the words which I and others use to refer to them. I have never forgotten a lesson learned in my mid-teens when my boyfriend and I argued for a couple of hours about the need for and value of 'democracy', before I realized that he was talking about Athens and I about America!

So that is where I have to start. For example, 'sin' is, in my experience, a very big word indeed, loaded with associations, most of them unpleasant and many of them unacceptable in our present society. A sixth-form religious instruction teacher told me that it was almost impossible to use the word in her class, since all of the pupils understood it in a condemnatory, fundamentalist sense which half of them accepted as the basic framework for their lives and the other half vigorously repudiated. Many people do not, and do not want to, think in such denigrating and loaded terms, and so they reject the word itself.

There is the further problem that, like the word 'immorality', 'sin' has become almost synonymous with sexual wrongdoing. A person who recognizes his or her own greed or envy might well resist its being called a sin, because, after all, it is not being expressed sexually; or might not consider himself even to be a sinful person because the corroding discontent and resentment which he fosters in himself are not about sexual matters. This confusion and limitation are very unfortunate, because the accurate recognition of sin is important in all the aspects of human life.

A lot of words change their meaning so completely that we simply have to accept their present unsuitability, and find new words and phrases for our ideas. But we should not let words go without a fight for them. We are under some obligation to examine how they have been used in the past, and to ask whether they could be used again in that traditional sense, or re-used with an altered but clarified meaning, rather than just given up. For this book, I will try to rehabilitate the word 'sin', first by looking at its previous and present use and then by relating it to our experience, and to reach a definition which I hope you will find valid.

The Hebrew word from the Old Testament which is usually translated as 'sin' did not carry the sense of condemnation with which we are familiar. It meant 'to miss', such as missing the mark in archery, or missing the road when travelling – and how apt that is for our theme. But for many centuries, western Christians at least have given the word a powerfully negative significance. Gerard Hughes SJ, in *God of Surprises*, refers to the 'false notions of sin and repentance' to be found in the Christian churches, where

> bad teaching in the institutional stage of religion can leave the impression on children's and adults' minds that God, in his infinite mercy, has sown a thick minefield in this vale of tears, [and] entrusted the minefield's map only to the teaching authority of the Church . . . The damage done to a sensitive and imaginative person by this kind of teaching is tragic and a perversion of the Good News.[1]

## SIN AND GUILT — AND CHOICE

I have quoted Hughes here exactly because he is a committed member of a Christian church and his opinion cannot be dismissed as that of a disaffected rebel unwilling to make the effort of resisting sin. Sin is painful enough, heaven knows, and the struggle against it is difficult and confusing, but perhaps not entirely for the reasons and in the ways which the churches have taught.

The traditional meaning of the word 'sin' has been wide but not at all vague. As the New Testament puts it: 'To commit sin is to break God's law: sin, in fact, is lawlessness.'[2] By the fourth century, Augustine was even more precise and no less wide: 'Any thought, word, or deed against the law of God'. Our great-grandparents held the same view, although by now there was an indication of the importance of choice, as my oldest dictionary indicated in 1895: 'Any voluntary transgression of the law of God . . . not only actions, but neglect of known duty . . . and all that is contrary to the law of God. It may consist of commission, when a known divine law is violated, or in omission, when a positive divine command . . . is voluntarily and wilfully neglected.'

Thus, in the traditional view, to break God's law is the core of sin; and there has been no shortage of instruction on the law, though it is necessarily accompanied by literally endless complications and subtleties about how the law must be applied and interpreted in actual situations. Hughes' comment is amusing:

> Alongside this teaching there developed a most complex casuistry to enable the pilgrim people of God to know how near they might approach to a minefield without actually being blown up. Deliberately missing Mass on Sundays was a mortal sin, but if you lived more than three miles walking distance from the church, or if you were ill, or you were a farmer and would lose your crop if not harvested immediately, or you were likely to meet someone at Mass who might be a serious occasion of sin, then you could be excused from the obligation![3]

Even when the laws of God seem very clear, applying them to

daily life, with or without the guidance of a church, is a most inexact art. The simplest law of all, 'Love the Lord your God with all your heart, with all your soul, with all your mind', goes on to a second half, 'and love your neighbour as yourself', which has been, indeed has to be, reinterpreted in every generation.

The essence of Old Testament law is supposed to be contained in the ten commandments, and is specific. Idolatry and blasphemy and defiling the sabbath are sins, as are murder, adultery, stealing and perjury. By implication, failing to honour one's parents is also a sin. These are all external acts, and coveting a neighbour's possessions is an act, albeit an internal one (and hinting at an internal state); so they all could, in theory, be clearly known and clearly, however painfully or reluctantly, avoided. I, for one, do not find this helpful. I am not tempted to murder or theft; I would rather avoid adultery for a number of reasons, and I dislike lying. To me all time is holy, whenever it falls within the week, and not to be defiled, but that particular commandment does not seem to be referring to the many petty ways in which I waste this gift. I can, and sometimes even do, take to heart the injunction against coveting what others have and I do not, but this is precious little support or instruction to take away from the most famous ten points of our religious history. In fact, I have never found teaching about the 'laws of God' to be much guidance in distress or support in effort, at all.

Nevertheless, I do not want to sound scornful. Countless millions of people have found such guidance and support, and great numbers still do. It has been important to the moral basis of our society, and a great many profound minds have been devoted to it. For many people it *is* guidance; and, to carry forward our image, I want to suggest that it is *guidance for pilgrims*, in the sense I used before. The laws describe the sort of person which they say God wants one to be, and all the commentaries and instructions map out the way to achieve this aim. They are usually the first map which we have, and they will never be completely irrelevant, however much we each have to amend the details as we make our own journeys.

The seven deadly, or mortal, sins have been common themes of sermons, art and literature since the Middle Ages. They seem to me to be important as inner states of sin, in which sinful acts are bred. Pride, anger and envy are more likely nowadays to be called attitudes, or personality traits, out of which harmful and unpleasant actions arise; if severe, they might even fall into a category of personality disorders. This would seem to make the deadly sins more helpful to the thinking of modern pilgrims than the commandments are; and although on the whole they have gone out of fashion as a theme, they do form a bridge between legalism and more interior definitions of sin. Certainly one could never claim to be loving God with heart and mind while harbouring pride or anger, and one is highly unlikely to love one's neighbour very much either, so there is no conflict between this schema and that primary law; and I shall have reason to come back to it later.

Basic to these traditional views of sin is the concept of original sin, which to most people nowadays is either ludicrous or horrendous. It is claimed to be the condition of sinful corruption into which every person is born, because we are all descendants of Adam, the first to break God's law, and we therefore share his ineradicable guilt. If you do not believe that Adam was our direct ancestor, you cannot believe this, however black your view of human nature; and a very great many people object vigorously or suffer piteously because they are told that they are inescapably and ineradicably sinful. The language of the Church of England is, in fact, moderate: '. . . man is very far gone from original righteousness, and is of his own nature inclined to evil.'[4] Who could disagree that we are 'inclined' to evil? The results are around us, personally, socially and globally, all the time. And many might even agree that it is 'of our own nature', without being able to ascribe that nature to descent from Adam. John Hick speaks from within our modern scientific view: 'For it seems to be a fact that humans emerged within the process of biological evolution as intelligent animals, programmed to seek their survival within a harsh environment, and thus with a basic self-regardingness which is the essence of "sin"',[5] but even this is contradicted today by studies which emphasize the co-operative nature of the earliest hunting groups and hunter/gatherer clans. Like so many other issues, the question of whether humankind is inherently and centrally sinful can be argued strongly on either side, and the fact that the western churches have argued 'Yes' for so many centuries does not free us from having to answer for ourselves.

As a rabid middle-of-the-roader, I am bound to agree with Erich Fromm's reasonable conclusion:

> Man *is* neither good nor evil. If one believes in the goodness of man as the only potentiality, one will be forced into rosy falsification of facts, or end up in bitter disillusionment. If one believes in the other extreme, one will end up as a cynic and be blind to the many possibilities for good in others and oneself. A realistic view sees both possibilities as real potentialities, and studies the condition for the development of either of them.[6]

But as a Quaker, I believe 'there is that of God in everyone'.[7] God is within us, and wherever, as individuals, personalities and souls, we touch upon that we are good. The core is sound and sweet, however the flesh is bruised, unripe or cankered. The 'basic self-regardingness' is not always frailty, it is sometimes downright badness; but it is not, I believe, the most basic part of us. It is undeniably the part we most often choose, but we almost always do have some degree of choice, and that is what this book is about. 'The tendency to follow the worst despite perceiving the better', Christopher Bryant said of original sin.[8] The more clearly and steadily we perceive the better, the less likely we are willingly or knowingly to follow the worst. We may fall into it often and often, that is our woundedness, but we are less likely to choose it, which is what constitutes our sin.

## New paths of righteousness

As I look at these definitions, I have been steadily moving away from the traditional viewpoints towards a more modern outlook. Explaining Charles Williams' theology, thirty years ago, Mary Shideler refers to eternal goodness and says, 'Sin means departure from that goodness in any direction and for any reason'.[9] Here there is still the wide coverage of Augustine's 'thought, word, and deed' but no reference to law; and my most recent dictionary defines sin as 'the condition of estrangement from God arising from a transgression of His will', the first lexical reference to the quality of estrangement which is to be found so often now in writers or speakers, and among our friends, and in our own experience. Estrangement, separation, departure, distance – these are the words we hear; they are the ones I use.

The emphasis has moved from our sinful acts to the experience we have of a disturbed or even damaged relationship with God – towards goodness, or reality, or authenticity, even if we are not the sort of people who usually think in terms of having a 'relationship with God'. We are distressingly aware that our inner being is awry, and we know or sense that it is because we have lived wrongly; we sense or can see that because of it we do wrong things, or at the least things which go wrong when we attempt them. Something has to be realigned in us, though we are hard put to say what; we are not on the right road, because we can feel that we are coming no closer to what we hunger for. I think that we are hungering for righteousness. That is a word which most of us reject because it can hardly be heard without the unspoken prefix 'self-', but it is such a beautiful word:

> ... The compassionate love of God that forgives sin is no other than God's love of his own righteousness, for the sake of which and through the love of which he makes man righteous again ... This righteousness ... is nothing else but the unalterable purity and perfection of the divine love which, from eternity to eternity, can love nothing but its own righteousness, can will nothing but its own goodness, and therefore can will nothing towards fallen man but the return of his lost goodness by a new birth of the divine life in him, which is the true forgiveness of sins.[10]

Who would not want such righteousness! I hope this is a word I can re-habilitate. When we are awry, when the path we are on is out of alignment with the path of reality and fulfilment which God offers us, then we ache to find ourselves back on the 'path of righteousness', to be among those who honour the right.

This internal state of aching need is increasingly the focus for those who examine the actual experience of sin. It is not by accident that I have come back to the imagery of the path. I feel that when we have moved away from conventional teaching about laws and actions we have as a result left the pilgrim's path, and as we become more aware of inner states, of relationship, of the complexities of choice, we become explorers. We start to make our own path as we try, with stumbling and pain, to align our lives with God's right path for us. It seems that separation must be an inevitable experience for some of us, either separation from others who appear to know exactly what the path should be and that we should be on it, or the painful sense of estrangement from our selves and from God if we do not explore the unknown country which is opening for us. Do not be disheartened. There is an old story of a pilgrim to Mecca who could not find any road which would take him to the holy place. He set himself to make one, picking up the stones that littered the desert and laying them one by one as they fitted best. He laboured ceaselessly, bent over with aching back or down on hands and knees fitting stones to make a road so that he could start for Mecca at last; until one day he looked up from his task to see, with humble joy, that he had finished building the road and had reached the shrine.

Through all our effort and struggle, however we fail or fear, we are not inherently separated from God. We cannot be, because he is within us. We have difficulty in believing this, we cannot feel it, we do not know how to become aware of it – *that* is original sin; but it is our faulty perception, not the true situation. What is more, we cannot even, really, separate ourselves from him; we can only do things which make us feel separate, or lead us to believe that we are separated – and, for as long as it lasts, that feeling is real.

## My definition at last

I want to stress this point about our choice and action. A group of my friends who have been studying the *Revelations* of Julian of Norwich spent an evening discussing her views of sin, and their own.

One of them said, 'My sense of sin derives from my sense of purpose. I think that what I'm here for, what all human beings are here for, is to grow and to embody more of God; and sin is anything I do which impedes that in me or in anybody else.'[11] She felt that there was not enough recognition, even in Julian, as there had not been in our tradition, of the good impulse in us to grow and to embody God, but she was also firm that sin is not something that just happens, and everyone present agreed. Though none of them regularly used the word 'sin' for it, the experience of awareness, choice and consequences was a reality. There are many people who do not even think in any 'religious' terms at all, for whom it is a reality; and I would like to carry the idea of impeding the embodiment of God one step further and to suggest, at last, my own, explorer's definition of sin: 'That which avoidably damages or diminishes your own or another's *livingness*'. This most precious quality is the vitality and responsiveness within people, relationships and situations, their most essential source of growth and gladness.[12]

The use of the word 'sin' here covers sinful, damaging acts, and also states of sin, namely, attitudes, orientations or persistent intentions which are always most centrally damaging to one's own livingness, and which may well be damaging to others as well. There are three essential points in the definition. The sin is *avoidable*. Honest mistakes, however harmful, are not sins; we all do many wrong things, in fear or ignorance, or sometimes even in selfishness or stubbornness, which I would not call sin. They are made in some ignorance of the situation, and it is to be supposed that if we had had greater knowledge we would have chosen to use it and would have avoided the action or attitude. Nor is failure the same as sin. Determining which is failure and which sin in our lives is one of the most difficult and uncertain tasks of conscience and self-knowledge, but there undoubtedly is a radical difference. After my father's death when I was three, my mother put me into a foster home and moved to a large city to find work, taking with her all of our small family, including my grandmother and aunt. This eighteen-month 'desertion' was damaging enough to me, goodness knows, but at the time my mother was shocked, grieving and bewildered, and her failure and error were not sin, in my mind. On the other hand, I was taken out of high school when I turned seventeen, though already being prepared for university scholarships, and sent out to work, because my earning capacity helped to disguise the fact that my mother was actually living with a man who ostensibly only shared our house. I appreciate that in 1949 there were considerable pressures to hide adultery and cohabitation; nevertheless, she could have avoided this stifling of my whole career at no cost to herself except that of her conventional self-esteem. That, therefore, was sin.

The second point is that it is *damaging* or *diminishing*. Externally, this would mean that the conscious or unconscious purpose of the action was to cause damage to another; though a sin may not always succeed in doing so. A person may intend to harm another, or to gain some advantage at another's cost – jealously to undermine a young person's confidence before a first date or an important interview; to harass an unwanted neighbour with noise, filth and threat; to obtain a bullying power over a child; to lie about a colleague's sexual behaviour – but will fortunately fail, because of circumstances, or of strengths in the intended victim. There is still a victim, though, and still the damage of sin, for the sinner at least is most terribly damaged, perhaps in conscience, certainly in selfhood and spirit.

Finally, it damages or diminishes *livingness*. In my examples, what is harmed is the expansion of personality, the enjoyment of a family in their home, a child's dependence and trust, a worker's satisfying achievement; all are vital springs of livingness. The damage can be much more serious, much more terribly extensive, I know, than in these homely instances; but in that case it is also more likely to be evident. I am interested in the small, vicious, persistent sins. I knew a woman, slightly disabled and often ill, who looked forward with eagerness to weekend car excursions into the country; but they were almost always spoiled by one thing or another going wrong, to spark complaint and argument. It took her a very long time to realize that her husband, far from being anxiously disappointed as he seemed, was actually obtaining a sly satisfaction out of her spoilt pleasure. That is sin.

The philosopher Simone Weil wrote, 'That which gives more reality to beings and things is good, that which takes it from them is evil.'[13] For me, reality is the very central rightness of life, the most vibrant, truest alignment of our selves and our actions with God's pattern of grace. When we feel that 'everything fits', that our inner being and the outer universe are in complete harmony, however fleetingly, when we know that what we are and what we are doing have their right place in the pattern, though it may be a hard or painful one – that is reality. It is the centre-most spring of our being. It feeds the livingness which makes life gracious and strong; and whatever takes reality from beings and things is sin. Sins steal livingness from us when we are its victims; it blocks reality from us when we are sinners.

I have said that coveting is the only internal action in the ten commandments, I called the seven deadly sins attitudes or internal states, and have distinguished between attitudes of sin and sinful actions. These points lead up to the relationship between separation and livingness. When we cannot see or believe in, especially cannot trust, God's goodness, we feel ourselves to be separate from him. In this grey half-life, we conspire for our own egotistical advantage or we fight against the reality offered to us, and fall into actual sin. Then, without respect for livingness or longing for it, we do not respond to God's life in us, and a state of sin becomes fixed; from here we strike out at livingness wherever we perceive it, and our alienation becomes complete. We know nothing except estrangement, from God, self and others. This is a vicious (a vice-ious) circle – one which I hope is not well established in my readers! The struggle which we are considering is indeed an attempt to prevent it from becoming strong, and we will look for ways to break into it, later on.

Clearly, with a definition like that, 'sin' remains a big word, referring to very serious acts and conditions. Most of what we do wrong, however, is not that important or harmful; but rather than resort to the traditional distinction between serious, mortal sins and less significant venial sins I would rather use the old-fashioned term 'wrongdoing' for the latter and reserve the word 'sin' for those acts and states which truly damage livingness. But sometimes it seems to be a very flexible boundary, which needs a lot of examination. I think it could be said that wrongdoing affects only the material circumstances, or the surface of the personality, without either deep or lasting consequences – small lies, petty unfairness, minor cheating, casual criticism. We all, without exception, do things like this. If I were willing to accept the formulation that we are all 'miserable sinners', it would be on this ground. Instead I prefer to call us wrongdoers – to begin with, it sounds more manageable! By whichever name, though, I believe that it too has to be understood and resisted, because of those flexible, even ambiguous, boundaries. Wrongdoing is a territory that can extend almost imperceptibly, to become a source of more harmful sin, and it is one whose consequences can suddenly become serious.

In the Julian study group I mentioned, another friend emphasized the element of choice, expanding it into awareness: 'I think that sin is a *deliberate* act which is going to hurt somebody; and I am beginning to think that another kind of sin is an almost deliberate act of unawareness, a choice not to be aware.'[14] Erich Fromm carries the thought further: 'Most people fail in the art of living not because they are inherently bad or so without will that they cannot live a better life; they fail because they do not wake up and see when they stand at a fork in the road and have to decide. They are not aware when life asks them a question, and when they still have alternative answers.'[15] My own opinion is that the lack of awareness is often sin and is often used to camouflage sinful acts, and I am certain that it always makes people more susceptible to sin.

## SIN AND GUILT — AND CHOICE

We dull ourselves to the spiritual consequences of physical and psychological acts. Usually we are aware only of the material and some of the emotional consequences, which we can observe; and many of our actions do not have much significance beyond this anyway. But some of them have a spiritual dimension — and we often do not know beforehand which ones these will be. This is sometimes why an apparently minor action can have enormous consequences for someone else. After such an occasion, we may of course say to ourselves that we merely touched on a raw emotional nerve in the other person, out of all proportion to what we did; this is one of the possibilities we have to sort out in our minds afterwards. But maybe, instead, it did have a deeper hidden influence, upon their spiritual life or their central being, perhaps without their even being able to realize it.

Hidden effects like these can arise out of the sacramental quality of life. A sacrament is the outward and visible sign of an inward and spiritual grace — and its mirror image is the visible sign of an inward evil. Our sins may, and probably do, have consequences far beyond any perceptible physical or emotional effects; and even though we may have been ignorant of this dimension, and did not spiritually intend those consequences, they have happened nevertheless. It is essential to know oneself and the depth of one's actions, and to be aware of the extent of what happened because of them. Examination of conscience is not just 'What did I do?' but also 'What did I cause to happen?'

This is not entirely bad news. The realization that our outward actions can have such harmful consequences is pretty hard to take, but the opposite realization is also true, and welcome — that although our good, our constructive, loving actions may seem small, their effects can be far deeper than the action itself could ever have suggested. The whole reason for the pilgrimage is to become the sort of person and to live in the sort of place where all one's actions *are* sacramental because they arise from the deepest springs of our reality. It is therefore essential that we know about our harmful actions and intentions, and learn how to refrain from them or to redeem them, so that our life on that level may be creative, not destructive.

## The gift of guilt

The struggle with sin requires an understanding of guilt, because they are not at all the same thing; and we cannot even begin to wrestle with guilt until we understand it a little. We may be so confused and hampered on our journey that we are hardly able to progress at all, if we either fail to recognize and acknowledge authentic guilt, which is the consequence of some real wrongdoing or sin, or are entangled by inauthentic guilt which has been instilled in us or absorbed by us.

Authentic, or justified, or rational, guilt is an appropriate, even a required, response when we have done something wrong and harmful, if we knew that it was so and knew what we were doing. It is a justified response also if we *believe* that we have done so, on the basis of the facts of what we did do, though perhaps according to standards which are not widely shared. (They may be hard-won individual standards, or those of a minority group; in either case, a majority group may claim that we are guilty and should feel it – but this is not the place to follow such ramifications.) Harry Guntrip wrote that 'rational guilt is felt realistically by a strong ego and faced, and reparation made for the wrong done. The guilt can then die away.'[16] I would call this the response of a true and mature conscience. In this sense, guilt is as necessary as pain. It is a warning sign that something is wrong, just as pain warns us of illness or injury. How dreadful if we never even knew we had really done wrong! How could it ever be made right? 'Unpleasant though it may be,' says Scott Peck, 'the sense of personal sin is precisely that which keeps our sin from getting out of hand. It is quite painful at times, but it is a very great blessing because it is our one and only effective safeguard against our own proclivity for evil.'[17] When the harm is specific and reparation can be made, guilt nags us uncomfortably until we do it. This is its straightforward function. The solution may not be easy, as we shall explore later, but it is clear; and to continue in guilt

## SIN AND GUILT – AND CHOICE

without attempting a reformation of our actions would be in itself a sin.

Even having to admit that we are 'guilty' is often somehow a little easier than having to 'take the blame' for the consequences of an action. There is something close to the bone, something very personal, about blame, or about being told that it is 'your fault', perhaps because it is ordinary, daily language which we have used since childhood, without the intellectual remove of courtrooms and official justice. We can sometimes know that we are guilty of a particular action, may even be able to admit to ourselves that we are, but will rear in fury and denial if somebody then says that we are therefore to blame for the consequences. There is a sharp psychological difference between private admission and confession, and admitting before others that one is to blame for some wrong. Like alcoholics at last facing an AA group, we have to learn to say, 'I am to blame for what happened'. That is when the change starts; that is why guilt nags.

For the sinner who never seems able to reach this cauterizing point, who has wrestled with sin until the sense of self-worth is crumbling, justified guilt is an even deeper, paradoxical blessing, because it is the pain which our innermost goodness feels when it has been repudiated. We would not feel guilty if we were not already, somewhere inside ourselves, good in greater degree than we have sinned. Our ability for goodness is exactly what is feeling guilty; our very guilt says something marvellous about our goodness. If guilt is seen as a sign of weakness, to be denied or hidden, it causes sterility in action, and a loss of self-respect in feeling. But admitting to real guilt is a sign of strength and the capacity to mature; it opens up a forward movement.

When we have really looked at our sin or justified guilt, we suffer the pain of what we could be or are asked to be, and we yearn for the wholeness which our sin withholds from us. The loneliness of feeling separated from God, the longing for our real selves which guilt can uncover for us, are a crossroads on our journey, and a signpost to the way ahead. We can use the energy locked up in real guilt to repent and to transform our lives, so that this real burden will be lifted from us.

Sin and its justifiable guilt are inextricably joined. In all the rest of this book, whatever I say about sin is true also, in only slightly different ways, of authentic guilt which has arisen from actual wrongdoing and sin.

## Hagridden and hounded

*In*authentic, unjustified guilt is perhaps even more common and persistent, and is the cause of grinding misery. Disparagingly called 'imaginary guilt', this feels very real and is terribly painful and frightening. But it also feels inescapable, because we do not know *how* to repent. We do not have any idea what our sin was, and we mentally rake over all our actions to find the answer. Or we may feel guilt even when it could be widely agreed that we did not do anything to justify such a harrowing response, or even when neither we nor anyone else knows of anything at all we have done that might have caused it. Even further, we may also feel guilt when someone else says that what we have done was wrong, even though we ourselves do not believe it to have been so. We may know in our hearts that we have not done wrong, though we are accused, or we can believe that whatever it is we have done is not as blameworthy as others claim; so we do not know what we can do to put matters right, or we sense that to do what is demanded of us will be a form of self-betrayal. None of these conditions should be called merely 'guilt', which would validate a claim that 'sin' must be present somewhere. They all need an adjective – they are 'unjustified', 'unrealistic', 'exaggerated', or 'induced' guilts.

They may germinate in a deep wound in the personality. Harry Guntrip offers the example of a child who is 'afraid to face the fact that he is not loved by his parents and finds it easier to conclude that it is he himself who is all wrong'.[18] The child says, in effect, 'Since they don't love me it *must* be because I have done something really awful.' And what the child concludes the adult later believes; such a person grows up willing to believe anything bad about himself or herself.

Unjustified guilts are also likely to arise from harsh and denigrating standards which a person has incorporated without ability or opportunity to assess them. A child has to accept the opinions of itself which are reflected from others, and if what he or she most frequently receives are criticism, complaint and blame, these are absorbed, often in a distorted and exaggerated form, into a part of the mind which just becomes a hidden imitation of the angry or belittling parents and teachers. This is the 'super-ego', and the person afflicted by it is hagridden all through life, unless grace and human help intervene to provide a more realistic basis for standards and choices. It is useful during the learning stages of life as a carrier of conventional norms, but can often be a remorseless dictator in adulthood, especially if it was formed out of impossibly high standards, the undermining of self-respect with ridicule and criticism, or condemnation of independent action. It must be clearly distinguished from the true conscience which warns us of actual wrong doing and sin and is the real, individual voice of a person's own firsthand experience.

There is another, related distinction which arises from early wounding – the difference between unjustified guilt and a profound fear of punishment. An abused child may escape self-blame and guilt, may even have a positive sense of *not* having done wrong, but nevertheless grow up knowing that it is going to be punished. In the adult this becomes a fixed expectation for which the person constantly and unsuccessfully seeks a justification. The ability to discriminate between this feeling and real guilt is essential. In chapter 3 I will be looking at some of these wounds and their effects.

As if the subject were not already sufficiently complicated, unjustified guilt must be further divided, for in addition to the personal, psychological guilts we have just looked at, there is the 'existential guilt' of being human, the basic sense of being awry, and wrongly aligned, which we considered as original sin. Whether or not this is called 'sin', it is certainly widespread, probably universal. But in my experience, when the specific notes of our real and our unjustified personal guilts have been identified, the particular timbre of this one stands out as a deeper issue altogether.

But how can we know whether our guilt is authentic or not? In most cases of real guilt we are likely to know fairly easily. Many actions are widely agreed to be wrong, and we know if we have committed them. There are other actions which, though not generally condemned, so offend against our own standards that our personal guilt regarding them is clear and justified. The puzzlement arises when we cannot see any cause for our undeniable sense of guilt, or can see so many causes that it would be unreasonable to believe them all; it arises when we are accused, by implication or explicitly, of harmfulness and dishonesty and selfishness which we fear may be true, which we may even believe most of the time, but which something stubborn though frightened, something authentic, inside of ourselves will not accept. If we live the guilt which has been foisted upon us, in order perhaps to buy the favour or the so-called happiness of parents or spouse or even child, we are not true to ourselves. We have accepted the role of villain and deep inside ourselves we know that we are betraying our innocence, and are evading our true responsibility for bringing the real situation into the open. This can be the case even when we are not consciously aware of what the real situation may be; it can be the case when the two guilts are so intermingled that we are conscious only of guilt without being able to sense its source, and we consciously accept the name which others have given to it.

The first step towards discernment is to acknowledge guilt which is authentic by our own personal standards or by more objective standards which we accept, and then to follow the admission with willing repentance and reparation. A clear and humble conscience about the wrongdoing and sin which we are honestly able to understand becomes a source of light and strength in the more obscure and tangled guilts. These are so inextricably bound up with family relationships, with cultural standards which we have been taught or have absorbed unconsciously, and with contemporary pressures, that the injunction to 'know thyself' is imperative. Sometimes in the struggle to understand our own actions and motives, we find that the guilt was indeed inauthentic but what is uncovered by its removal may be just as unwelcome. We may have to admit, for example, to a weakness which would rather accept guilt than stand up to other people with a charge of their injustice, or at the other end of the spectrum to a terrifying anger which was only camouflaged by guilt and apology. I believe that our path is discernible, and it can be travelled because we are supported by grace; but I also know that it has some unwelcome surprises and many pains.

Inauthentic guilt is not the subject of this book. With sympathy and understanding of its problems, I must therefore leave it aside. When I refer to guilt from now on, it will be to justified guilt arising from real (though perhaps still hidden and denied) wrongdoing and sin.[19]

## Re-spondere

But I cannot leave the subject of guilt without saying something about responsibility. It is sometimes very difficult to make people realize that they are not the same thing. So touchy is their self-esteem that if they are held responsible for anything they think that they are being blamed, are being told it is their fault and that they should feel guilty. But our law distinguishes between the two, when a person causes a death: if he intended it, he committed murder; if not, the charge is manslaughter. In both cases the person is dead, and he is responsible for the death; but in one case culpably so, and in the other case, ignorantly or even, in a sense, innocently.

It is almost as though many people cannot recognize any difference between responsibility and culpability. They therefore cannot, almost dare not, admit responsibility; which means that they cannot feel or often even be responsible, and cannot grow into the mature benefits of being responsible. 'Responsibility' at root derives from the Latin *spondere*, to pledge. A person who has given a pledge must answer, must give a response, that it has indeed been carried out. To be responsible is to be answerable, to say 'I did do it'. Whereas 'culpable' –

from *culpa*, meaning fault – is defined as 'deserving censure, blameworthy'. Who would want to be culpable? But who, able to make the distinction, would not want to widen and deepen their sense of responsibility?

I have suffered from my own version of this widespread confusion, and do not feel at all superior to those who are caught in it. I know exactly the day when I was finally freed of it, in November 1964, when my journal notes quietly: 'The full realisation that there are errors of innocence and burdens laid upon it, which carry responsibility but *no guilt*'. I did do it; oh dear heaven, yes, I did it. I have never been able to repair the harm – and that still hurts. But I was not guilty, for I did not know anything better and could not have done anything else at that time.

There are burdens laid upon innocence. A person innocent of all ill-will or bad intention *may nevertheless* – perhaps even ignorant of the real situation – do something which has harmful consequences. That person, though innocent, though not culpable, is still responsible for that act and to some extent for the results, and is responsible for making any reparation that is possible. It is desperately sad if reaction against feeling or seeming guilty prevents the individual from admitting the harm and having the chance to make it good. It is a shame, also, if somebody will not undertake some endeavour lest failure would make him or her guilty, rather than responsible.

Many people, able to make this distinction, will not feel guilty but will accept the responsibility for their act and its consequences, and will want to make some reparation or will regret that this is not possible. If something is our fault, if we are to blame, then we must face our guilt. But if something bad comes about because of our failing, or our weakness – well then, indeed, it is a bad something, but we are responsible, not guilty. Who should blame us, rather than pity us, for the weakness that brought such a failure?

## Black refusal

The ultimate sufferer from sin is the sinner. Grace Jantzen says that Julian of Norwich 'considers sin to be the most grievous of all the pains we have to bear, because it fractures our personality and sets our sensuality against our godly will which is united to God . . . This internal fracture and the suffering it causes Julian considers to be the worst of all suffering and in some sense the cause of all the rest.'[20] Sinners are wounded people. Sometimes the wounds prompt the sins; certainly the sins leave wounds. Though we must not refrain from judgement of the harmful acts of sin, in most cases compassion will be our best guide to understanding, and forgiving, the state which prompted them, whether this is in others or ourselves; and almost everything that I have to say will be from this viewpoint.

But there is one subject I must look at now which has to be handled differently. It is rather less a matter of wounds than of poison, and is truly terrible. There are some cases where a warm and loving compassion in a friend or relative of the sinner, though the right first attitude, will prove mistaken or be exploited, and one then has to develop a different quality which is hard to name – perhaps 'stern compassion'.

During most of my life I had no experience of evil. I respected the honesty of those who claimed to, but could not understand. But eventually I came into contact with something which I called The Blackness, and I spoke of 'contagion'. I still did not say 'evil' – that was such a terrible word to use of someone I knew; until I read Scott Peck's courageous book on the subject, *People of the Lie*: 'It is not their sins per se that characterize evil people, rather it is the subtlety and persistence and consistency of their sins. This is because the central defect of the evil is not the sin but the refusal to acknowledge it.'[21]

The *refusal*. I began to understand; but I still questioned. I was deeply loath to call anyone 'evil'; if a person were truly unable to see the sin, would he or she be evil? No; for, in Peck's words, 'evil deeds do not an evil person make'.[22] But that reassurance could not last, for this person developed considerable insight into what was happening, and nevertheless continued to do it. Evil people can be defined, Peck said, 'by the consistency of their sins. While usually subtle, their destructiveness is remarkably consistent. This is because those who have "crossed over the line" are characterized by their *absolute* refusal to tolerate the sense of their own sinfulness.'[23] Yes, that is what I had been watching – the change from unwillingness to admit specific sins into the refusal to tolerate even any suggestion of sinfulness. Then I remembered reading, long before, in James Hillman's *Insearch: Psychology and Religion*, a passage which I had not been able really to understand but which had stuck in my mind because of its final sentence:

> The demonic or diabolic in itself is arbitrary, mischievous, often a matter of luck or lot . . . [but] when it is joined with the human ego, the will and reason and desire with which a man can choose a course of action and pursue an end, then does the merely devilish become truly evil. This implies that the archetypal shadow never achieves full actuality until it is linked in a pact with the human. And we are driven to conclude that the Devil too would incarnate in and through men.[24]

In these frightening quicksands, I found a footing upon Christopher Bryant's sane and experienced description in *The Heart in Pilgrimage*. He refers to first-century Christians who were 'writing out of their experience of a *mystery of iniquity* which it is folly to underestimate even if we describe it differently', and says:

> There is a psychic evil, a force destructive of humanity at work within the area of the psychic. The idea of the psychic is difficult to define. But there is mounting evidence, which few informed persons will dispute, of an unconscious interflow of ideas and impressions between individuals which appears to move independently of physical contact, of space, and perhaps of time . . . Some of this interflow appears to be evil and to destroy or disturb the mental balance of individuals . . . [25]

I am certain now that I have been in increasing contact with evil. I can use the word without feeling either foolish or outrageous, and I understand, with pain, when I read authors like those above, who know so much about this tragic subject. After these years of experiencing the black effects of evil actions, I believe that persistent sinners are frighteningly vulnerable to evil. They allow this force to have expression in the world through some of their sins, which then become different in kind, and not just worse, because of the change. They do evil things — sometimes — though they are not yet evil people. But that is a terrible vulnerability.

I am distressed and frightened by this power of evil, but I do still believe that, during a perhaps long period of vulnerability, it can be resisted and eventually defeated. Surely if anything would draw sinners away from sin, it is knowledge of The Blackness. Peck confirms the supreme value of self-awareness:

> More than anything else, it is the sense of our own sinfulness that prevents any of us from undergoing a similar deterioration . . . The poor in spirit do not commit evil. Evil is not committed by people who question their own motives, who worry about betraying themselves . . . [but by] the self-righteous who think they are without sin because they are unwilling to suffer the discomfort of significant self-examination . . . It is out of their failure to put themselves on trial that their evil arises . . . Evil originates not in the absence of guilt but in the effort to escape it.[26]

You see? Guilt *is* a blessing.

But the willingness, the effort and sacrifice, must not be delayed too long. Once past a certain gradient, the downward slide is hard to escape. Mary Shideler writes of 'the deliberate perversity which, if persisted in, destroys [a person's] capacity for distinguishing between good and evil, beauty and ugliness, love and malice'.[27] Peck, again, is the one who describes the state most uncompromisingly:

Forever fleeing the light of self-exposure and the voice of their own conscience, [evil people] are the most frightened of human beings. They live their lives in sheer terror. They need not be consigned to any hell; they are already in it . . . God does not punish us; we punish ourselves. Those who are in hell are there by their own choice. Indeed, they could walk right out of it if they so chose, except that their values are such as to make the path out of hell appear overwhelmingly dangerous, frighteningly painful, and impossibly difficult. So they remain in hell because it seems safe and easy to them. They prefer it that way.[28]

Are you, my fellow travellers, *wrestling* with sin and guilt? Be glad of that. You are not in hell; you are on a path, or want to know about a path, or believe there must be a path, which will lead to a place of goodness. That is already a choice away from hell. 'Man must choose between good and evil, blessing and curse, life and death. Even God does not interfere with his choice; he helps by sending his messengers . . . to warn and to protest. But this being done, man is left alone with his "two strivings", that for good and that for evil, and the decision is his alone.' Or hers.[29]

In sin we turn away from God, from our real selves, and from others. Sin is always the choice of the ego, setting itself and its needs and desires against God and the deep goodness of the real self to which it is only peripheral. Sin creates its own isolation, in this double separation; and the ego must accept a double forgiveness, from God and from the deep self, and accept a secondary position in the sinner's life, before isolation and the risk of evil can be left behind.

Teilhard de Chardin says that something is happening in the universe, a working out which is 'the birth of a new spiritual reality *formed by souls and the matter they draw after them*'.[30] We are creating a spiritual world, which Teilhard calls the 'noosphere', and I believe that evil is its shadow. *Spiritual* reality is formed by souls: evil is a dark *psychic* reality formed by perverted egos. That is why all the effort against sin, and each refusal of wrongdoing, is valuable. It is not only we who benefit from the lessening of our sin, but everyone in contact with us, for 'our hidden sins poison the air which others breathe'.[31]

## Choosing the current

Forgiveness and transformation are always possible, though sometimes the price in the surrender of egocentricity seems very high. Alan Jones calls conscience our 'homing instinct' – 'Love is the desire of every creature to find its proper place, to find its true home.'[32] The goodness of the real self never ceases to long for a harbour in the love of God and in harmony with others, and this possibility is always being offered to us. It seems to have been common in our tradition for writers and preachers to assume a static situation when considering humankind's fallen state or inauthentic existence; and they postulated a special action of God, as though he moved from where he had been in order to intervene at this spot and to change, with grace, a person's state.

But I believe that the opportunity to regain freedom is constantly being re-offered to people, in life's ceaseless flux and flow which is God himself always nearby, always touching and re-touching, always acting through always interacting individuals and events in every life. Now and then the opportunity and a person's ability meet, in the flow, and he or she again has a chance to move out of the imprisonment of wrongdoing or failure.

How mechanical, how almost dead, is that older, common view! There is a state of perfection: man falls and stays fallen; God moves in grace: man is drawn up. But I see a person's life with God as organic. It is as though we float or swim in a river, now rushing, now shallow, now with a dozen swinging currents, now fingering through marsh. Every time that the deep current and the carried object touch, God's inevitable flow of grace lifts the individual into the movement, if in response to the touch that person says, 'Yes'.

# 2

# TWO ETHICS

**Beginning with obedience**

We start our lives in the smallest community there is, our family, and for some years its standards are the only ones we know. We have no way of deciding, or even asking, whether or not these standards are 'right' – there are not any others to compare them with; and generally speaking we have to be obedient to them anyway because this community is our only means of survival and acceptance. It gradually widens, with the addition of other families, then with school and perhaps church, and (in our culture at this period) with the acquiring of information through reading and television; but the standards we absorb from it are unlikely to change very much during this early widening, they are rarely systematically expressed, and they cannot be seriously questioned. They form the 'ethic of obedience', the first and necessary framework for actions and beliefs. Many people will remain within it, comfortably, reluctantly, or exploitively; though most pilgrims-become-explorers will find themselves facing its limits and travelling into another beyond it.

I said in the previous chapter that it is the pressure to adhere to parental and community standards which develops the super-ego. In childhood and youth, what 'I' am taught is right or wrong by those 'above' me becomes a body of knowledge and injunction, (usually!) intention, and aspiration which is within me but is 'above' my ego. These internalized standards are all that we have to guide us during our early growth in the community, and I think that it is suitable to use the term super-ego for this period. In some cases they may remain the ones we hold to throughout our lives, perhaps because the 'hand-me-down' super-ego continues to command our thinking and action, a subject which forms part of the next chapter, or because we question and test them and decide that they do indeed continue to be valid for us. I like to use Tillich's term 'the socially produced conscience' for this latter stage, though not with the critical edge which he gives to it.[1]

It follows that what our community most values is likely to be the first goal of a pilgrimage. If we are the sort to journey at all, if we want personally to embody those social standards in our individual lives, then becoming the 'good' person which they define will be our goal. They will guide us in perplexity and determine our choices, and when we are in conflict between choices they will make demands on us. They remain the mores of our society, the customs and standards expected of us, but no longer merely accepted or followed unquestioningly. In this way they become an ethic, a more reasoned, perhaps even quite systematic, set of moral values by which we try to live.

John Sanford calls this the 'ethic of obedience',[2] which requires us to follow the commonly accepted standards of human conduct and relationship. Although it will not be the theme of this book, I do not want to disparage it. When it is really nothing more than submissiveness which is afraid to rebel and too lazy or dull to examine, it is a weak and unreliable ethic and likely to be accompanied by a number of sneakily unpleasant qualities. But true obedience will have wrestled with the reasons why and why not, and have reached a self-affirmation in its reaffirmation of the mores. As Harold Kushner says, 'It means knowing that some choices are good, and others are bad, and it is our job to know the difference.'[3] When we strive to follow the ethic of obedience, we learn to do that job.

Nevertheless, it can be difficult to find out clearly just what the goal of this pilgrimage is, and what is involved in being this sort of person. The community's standards may be expressed in sharp, clear injunctions which are, however, basically contradictory. One never knows when and how a great many of them were absorbed, and therefore cannot decide what weight to give to them. Even when they are specifically taught, there may be little help to consider them in the light of actual situations which arise. Years ago a friend of mine, a moderately devout Catholic with three children, started to use contraceptives. In this matter, she said, she had to turn to her own conscience, for the flat prohibition of her church did not make any allowances for their family resources, the sort of care she could give the children, and what seemed best when all the circumstances were taken into account. She knew that she was disobeying her own community, the Catholic Church, but she felt no sense of wrongdoing, much less of sin. I refrained from pointing out that she was thinking like a Protestant! But I certainly felt uncomfortable then with her position – if she was the one to decide which commands to obey and which not, was she being obedient at all?

Another reason why the goal is hard to imagine clearly is that the greater part of our background thinking and attitudes is formed by old rules and standards. We pick it up from old sayings and from literature (even at the level of childhood fairy stories), we learn old doctrines from an ancient source, we are given laws from earlier centuries and other societies. We learn, or at least hear, about the Ten Commandments, the Golden Rule, the Sermon on the Mount, the Seven Deadly Sins, scraps of Canon Law – and develop some very confused ideas about Original Sin and The Sin Against the Holy Ghost! But if people are pressed to look at what they really think, very few of them actually accept most of it at all wholeheartedly. They choose from it what they need for a particular decision, or to strengthen them in a course of action. In real conflict, they are likely to turn in great need to some particular part of it, especially if they have been specifically taught their standards in a religious setting; but even then, they tend to make individual decisions, as my Catholic friend did, without any very strong feeling of disobedience.

Very few people, either, could give any consistent account of what they believe to be right and wrong. Their standards usually form a sort of background to their lives, sufficient for most situations. But the trouble arises when they have to make exact choices, and do specific things, and hold to one particular line, on the basis of confused, contradictory or limited standards. This cultural background tends to be generally Christian, even in our 'post-Christian' world, and, too often, it is a Christianity which depicts a fallen mankind helpless to achieve redemption except through the action of someone 'out there'. How this relates to the responsibility 'in here' to respond to that action and to carry it forward is not, most often, a religious mystery for them but quite simply a puzzle – if indeed it is even thought about at all. Very much of most people's ideas of sin and the sense of guilt arises from a fall and redemption tradition which might have great folk power but is not understood even in its own terms. I am fortunate in being reminded often that my own thoughtful and moderately well-informed Quaker setting is a minute slice of the population, because I come into contact with university students of several ages and from other countries as well as the UK, and with people in the arts world. The proverbs, or the Golden Rule, or the implausible story of Adam's iniquity are threaded into the thinking of these intellectually able people without any ecclesiastical or theological matrix, and their ideas of Christianity will depend mainly upon chance – who they had happened to meet at some formative time, or what issues were getting television coverage.

When we were children, we needed rules, and perhaps most people continue to need them in adulthood; they give certainty and identity. Though obeying them can often be painful, it will usually not be confusing, it ensures us the safety and encouragement of the group, and enables us to avoid its sanctions. Remaining within the limits of what the community says is right or wrong can continue as long as our moral situation is stable. If there is not much change in our society, we will have to face only those problems in which its mores provide sufficient guidance. It will not matter that they may be vague or limited, as long as our lives present us with no sharp conflicts between standards nor with moral dilemmas outside their guidance.

But all of us live in a swiftly changing society now. Few of us have the safety of a small, closed community within that, and many have to move from the first, familiar communities to other very different ones. If it happens that we are members of a group which, effectively, decides for us, and we do not consider leaving it or are not forced to do so, our moral course may sometimes be very painful but it will be clear. However, few lives are so stable or fortunate, and the collective teaching breaks down or becomes inadequate for most of us. We cannot escape knowing about other moral standards, either, even if our community (and we with it) dismisses them as mistaken or wrong. We learn quite early that we live in a pluralist society. By the time we reach our teens most of us will have done some thinking about this; and during adolescence we will probably find ourselves in situations where we or our friends are faced with choices between different standards. We certainly cannot escape these situations forever. The teens and into early adulthood is the time when we either confirm our adherence to the mores of our community simply because it is ours, or we try to find a deeper and more enduring basis for our standards. We are then, in fact, trying to move beyond standards to values; we want to understand how the law is the expression of the will of God. We are developing our own awareness of what is right – in my terms, developing a socially produced (though not socially determined) conscience.

The struggle with guilt in the attempt to be obedient may often be the cause of growth into a deeper and more conscious obedience, as we attempt to fit our own experience, feelings and responses into the existing framework, trying either to change ourselves or to see beyond the mores merely as received standards and to integrate them into our own personal structure. The development of this wider ethical position may lead us into a new community where our early mores and our new ethics are in harmony. This may be in fact a new physical community, or it could well be the growing discovery of the cultural, moral and religious heritage of our present one, in the contact with more profound minds and the encouragement of our individual understanding. This has probably always been the primary aim of education, and for many people would surely still be the ideal.

## Early exploring

Perhaps you will see now why I compared the ethic of obedience with a pilgrimage, at least in the sense in which I am using that image. 'A pilgrim is going to a particular place, more or less by an accepted route.' Up until now, in my description, the person struggling with sin has been a pilgrim, and the 'holy place' has been described for him or her in terms of goodness, that is, as moral excellence – the quality of fulfilling well all those things which our own society asks of us. Probably, at the beginning of our life's journey most of us want to be pilgrims in this sense, and to set out for a known place – or at least to struggle towards it. But a lot of us founder or get lost as we travel. We try to return to the road, or to find our way cross-country to the intended shrine. Some of us make it. Some of us turn into explorers.

Of course, there have always been people who challenged accepted standards and doctrines. I am not trying to suggest that becoming an explorer is something new or particularly modern; but I do think that it is happening to more people than ever before, at least in our culture. For the rest of this book, mine will be an explorer's viewpoint; and what I shall be describing in the rest of this chapter is a struggle which results in new standards, or in the uncovering of different values out of which new standards will grow. Nevertheless, even the most creative and valuable change needs to occur in a setting of tradition or it becomes chaotic, and we must remember and respect that. The tension between the two is inevitable, but not undesirable, as Paul Tillich indicates:

> If love is the principle of ethics . . . how can a permanent uncertainty, a continuous criticism which destroys the seriousness of the ethical demand, be avoided? Is not law and are not institutions necessary in order to maintain the actual ethical process? Indeed, law and institutions are

required. They are required by love itself. For every individual, even the most creative, needs given structures that embody the experience and wisdom of the past, that liberate him from the necessity of having to make innumerable decisions on his own, and that show him a meaningful way to act in most situations . . . Love demands laws and institutions, but love is always able to break through them in a new *kairos*, and to create new laws and new systems of ethics.[4]

Quite a few years ago, I enjoyed frequent visits from a clergyman friend with whom I thrashed out a number of subjects. But about even more of them I got nowhere, because he was so often able to name my ideas as some particular heresy, and that put an end to the matter! I was blocked not only by his dogmatic certainty, but also by my own apologetic attitude towards 'the church' – though I had not even attended any particular church since I was seventeen. It is an attitude I only recently identified (for it is very subtle, evading intellect and burrowing into self-confidence) and I gladly gave it up, when as a new Quaker I realized that I was not only allowed but expected to think everything out for myself, and then encouraged to consider that it was, even so, only a personal and provisional conclusion. Now I am an unabashed Pelagian – like that fifth-century Celtic monk whom Rome declared heretical, I do not believe in original sin, whether inherited from Adam or just inherent in me, and I therefore do not believe that baptism is an essential first step to cleanse us of it. The ninth edition of the *Encyclopaedia Britannica* says: 'Whilst the Pelagians never existed as a sect separate from the Church Catholic, yet wherever rationalism has infected any part of the Church, there Pelagianism has sooner or later appeared.' I like that 'infected'!

I can be so light-hearted about it now because I have learned, in this and many subjects, that there are at least two thousand 'experts' in every one of them, and that having an authoritative opinion is largely a matter of choosing the experts who agree with you. Fortunately I did not have to battle against a vicar or minister or disapproving congregation, but I did have a long and lonely time working out where I stood; and so do a lot of other people. We are not heretics; we are just doing our own exploring. It is also called thinking for ourselves, and once Gutenberg had invented movable type it became inevitable.

A first step off the known way of the pilgrim, out of the ethic of obedience, is the need to question obedience itself. 'I was just obeying orders' has become one of the most horrifying statements of our age. We heard it at Nuremberg, and about My Lai; recent Dutch research with former torturers indicates that the larger number of them felt that they were simply 'doing their job'. Soldiers commit acts, as individuals, which the collective, through the chain of command, has told them to do. In the past, the collective absolved them of guilt for these acts, by its praise and medals, its claim of a 'just war', its respect for obedience. But after Vietnam, soldiers suffered their guilt as individuals because the collective would not, or probably no longer could, absolve them of it. Can the collective now, through any representative whatever, absolve any sins which it ordered? Can obedience ever again be an excuse? Surely now for the individual there has to be a personal line beyond which an act does not seem to him or her to be justified, and for which he will not accept even shared guilt.

I myself no longer feel comfortable with the idea of obedience even in the religious orders. Unquestioning obedience to authority would be appropriate only if the authority were going to be directly and fully responsible for the acts committed in its name. If the abbot were entirely responsible for the soul of a monk, or if an officer could be court-martialled for the consequences of an order the private carried out while the private is freed from blame and punishment, then obedience might rightly be asked of the monk and the private. But if a person has to carry the can for what he does, then he has the right to decide what can it will be. Intellectual authorities may well be correct, but they are rarely held responsible for what is done in their name – the doer is still left to decide, on his or her own authority and being personally responsible for the consequences, what to do. He or she therefore has the right, and I believe even has the obligation, to say, 'No, not that', even though the professors or the officers or the bureaucrats tell him what is so, or what to do.

Paul Tillich (clearly one of my own chosen 'experts') puts this stage of development more strongly than a need just to question:

> The decisive step to maturity is risking the break away from spiritual infancy with its protective traditions and guiding authorities. Without 'no' to authority, there is no maturity. This 'no' need not be rebellious, arrogant or destructive. As long as it is so, it indicates immaturity by this very attitude. The 'no' that leads to maturity can be, and basically always is, experienced in anxiety, in discouragement, in guilt feelings and despairing inner struggles . . . Much must be left behind: early dreams, poetic imaginations, cherished legends, favoured doctrines, accustomed laws and ritual traditions. Some of them must be restored on a deeper level, some of them must be given up.[5]

Once the questions, or the refusals, start, whatever they are about, they will not easily stop. Questions lead to choices, and decisions and actions. Life begins to change radically, standards to become unhelpful or irrelevant, and responsibility to take on a new significance. The questioning also leads to uncertainty. Within an ethic of obedience we can usually know fairly clearly what is a sin and whether we have sinned, or there is somebody who can work it out for us; and there is usually something clearly defined which can or must be done about it. But this all changes now. Not only is the time of decision itself uncertain, because there are so few guidelines, but the time afterwards also, when the results cannot be predicted and when the final outcome may even be largely unknown, or sometimes never be known to us at all.

'The Pauline overcoming of the law falls only to the man who knows how to put his soul in the place of conscience.'[6] In the terms I have used, it is the super-ego and the socially produced conscience to which Jung was referring, and it is what I would call the 'deep conscience of the soul' which must become the touchstone of obedience. Jung continue[s]... are capable of this. And these few tread this path... inner necessity, not to say suffering, for it is sharp... of a razor.' That was over sixty years ago. I believe... so-changed world (and not least because of the changes Jung brought to it) many more of us now feel this necessity, and undertake the risk.

The attempt to make a creative path through uncertainty and risk leads to a particular sort of growth. 'One mind develops where many merely adapt to circumstances.'[7] In this matter of sin and guilt, many people adapt to the existing mores and live within them, not finding their own values or making their own standards; others develop during the creative effort, which becomes a source of growth. When we struggle in this way to fit our own experiences, feelings and responses into the mores, and fail, when we try either to change ourselves or to find a wider context of values, then we begin to grow beyond what was given to us by our early community. It may be a pitting of ourselves against a large social pressure, or just a matter of standing against the view of a spouse or parent because we feel that we really must not go along with it. The small, personal situation is no less important, for that one person can be embodying the collective mores in this situation, and that one relationship becomes the locus of the whole struggle between two ethics.

Some often quoted words of George Fox are for me, as for others, a personal standard. Praising the scriptures as the prophets' words, and Christ's and the apostles' words, because they came directly from the spirit into their hearts, he continued, 'You will say, Christ saith this, and the apostles say this; *but what canst thou say*?'[8] In the end, we do, ourselves, make the decision about what to believe, about what is right and good, and what is sin. We may decide by default, because we never question what we have been taught or have absorbed; or we have the chance to examine that background actively, and to accept it consciously or to reject it and work out our own values. Only what *we* say, slowly and costingly, will enable us to grow out of sin and to put off the burden of guilt.

## The ethic of creativity

The terms 'ethic of obedience' and 'ethic of creativity' were probably coined by the Russian philosopher Berdyaev and were given a psychological meaning by John Sanford in *The Kingdom Within*. For me, they crystallized a conflict and an approach which had marked all my adult years. I was so reluctantly 'disobedient', I would very much have preferred the security and acceptance I badly needed from my family and then my marriage – but I could not live that way: literally, I could not have lived if I had continued on the paths I was first shown. A paragraph from Sanford's *The Man Who Wrestled with God* recently clarified my understanding of the path I *had* followed:

> There is also an ethic of creativity that requires us to be guided by our own inner truth. Then we do what we feel we must even though it runs counter to what is usually accepted. A person who departs from the usually accepted standards of behaviour puts himself or herself in a perilous position. It is too easy to fall into the trap of justifying the means by the end, and deluding oneself that since the goal of our behaviour was (in our minds) divinely sanctioned, the ends we chose were justified. All too readily this pose is simply another mask behind which to hide our selfish motives. Only a psychologically aware person, who truly knows himself or herself and especially the power motives, and is genuinely in touch with the divine purpose, can successfully follow the ethic of creativity. Only if a person knows what s/he is doing, accepts responsibility for what s/he is doing, and has come to terms with egocentricity so that the goals are not self-serving, can s/he depart from the ethic of obedience and follow the ethic of creativity. But when this does occur, the highest and most moral life of all is lived.[9]

Well, I would not want to be claiming that for myself! But I do know that a very individual life is lived, and almost certainly a difficult one, when we leave or lose the paths and have to start exploring. Dag Hammarskjöld asked the primary question:

'Do you create? Or destroy?'[10] The ethic of obedience, admittedly, is not often openly destructive, but it can be destructively inadequate in the twentieth century; and the more we question it and the more clearly we look at it, the more likely we are to see, with great dismay, its subtly undermining and hindering qualities. Within it, at best we only apply or re-apply solutions which were once somebody else's creation; but when it is we who do our own creating, we make something new and unique in our lives, a solution, or resolution, an initiative or a combination, which is for this particular situation in its wholeness.

The American Dominican Matthew Fox claims that the creation-centred spirituality, in which God had found all his creation good and asks from us rejoicing and blessing, is much older than the fall/redemption spirituality of radical sin and the necessity of a redemption which is offered to us from outside. In the latter, we avoid falling by obeying the law, and when we do fall we are redeemed by somebody else. Now we are returning to an emphasis upon creation, and in the ethic of creativity we must ourselves help in the process of our redemption. I believe that in this as in much else we are truly co-creators with God.

Once the ideal was perfection; now it is, I think, wholeness. Once the requirement was obedience, now it is collaboration. It could be said that the ethic of obedience is about goodness (and badness!) – if you obey the rules you are a good person; and perhaps it does not matter all that much how willingly or sincerely you obey them, because it is the action which counts, the obedience itself which matters. The ethic of creativity is more about wholeness and rightness. The ideal of this ethic is that at every moment, in every situation, there would be something to do which would be completely right because it was appropriate to the wholeness of the situation, including even its negative aspects. This 'most right thing' could not be the established law of God, but must be the whole unfolding pattern of his will in creation. We have seen that the law cannot cover every situation but must be qualified and elaborated if it is to fit all the changing details; in the ethic of creativity we accept this contingent quality, and work with it. We look for a perception of the whole pattern of creation and God's will, and for a way to fit into it creatively with as much of ourselves as we can open up and develop. The standard of decision and action is then how close we can come to God's rightness and wholeness for us, in spite of our human weakness and fallibility. Sin would therefore lie in the refusal or neglect to make the attempt, which matters more than any particular action; for though the action may in fact prove to have been mistaken or a failure, there is still the rightness itself to return to, and try again to conform ourselves to, in the next decision and action, and the next and the next. We become part of the flow of ongoing creation, sins changing in repentance and vision, failures undone in new commitments.

Clearly, if we choose to embark upon this way, or our lives force us to it, we each have to redefine sin, and sins. There will be times when the only right and whole course of action will involve doing what we have been taught is a sin. A friend of mine, a Christian with a deep commitment to the traditional view of marriage, had to question her own marriage after twenty-five years. There was a long struggle before she could admit that it was the marriage which was impeding God in her, and that the right and whole action was to leave it, a decision which cost her great fear and long guilt. 'I find it comforting to think that there is an ethic of creativity', she told me. 'I think I broke the ethic of obedience to my marriage vows — it does feel like going against the collective when you leave a marriage, because marriage *is* about the collective, at its roots. I had an enormous sense of disobedience, I felt very guilty for a couple of years. But I knew that I had chosen a creative life.'

One cannot leave sin and sins behind, you see; but the individual becomes the one with the responsibility for defining them as well as for avoiding or redeeming them. My friend had developed a different conscience. Paul Tillich uses a lovely phrase, saying that the conscience becomes transcendent in religion 'by the acceptance of the divine grace that breaks through the realm of law and creates a *joyful conscience*'.[11] We catch a vision of a new world, where the grey, gritty, heavy conscience of our struggle with sin and guilt becomes a joyful awareness of the pattern of grace and the wholeness of life.

Yet the ethic of creativity can be terrifyingly insecure. By its standards we cannot be quite sure whether or not we *have* sinned, because we can only know later, perhaps much later – sometimes, never at all – whether it worked out or not, whether we did damage to others or not, whether what seemed damage at the time was truly so or turned out to be a creative influence. If we are living by this ethic, a sense of sin in any conventional sense is almost irrelevant. There can be no contemporary objective standards: the only standards are the inner and outer consequences as they are seen over time, and the immediate feeling of appropriateness or necessity in the decision. We may of course fall short of the best we can do in that particular situation, but if we have tried to do the most right thing at that moment, and know that we have tried, then whether we fail or not, whether other people are hurt by it or not, is not a question of sin. It is a matter of failure and hurt and regret, and one may well be responsible for doing something about that; but it was not sin. Even if it should prove to have been a wrong decision, what matters is that it was made in full and prayerful consciousness. 'Whatever he chooses must be done with the consciousness of standing under an unconditional imperative.'[12]

It is clear that the new ethic, the way of the explorer, involves great risks. We may make bad mistakes, we will certainly be very lonely sometimes, we can never utilize an answer from anybody else and cannot always be sure of our own. There will be particular difficulty for the temperament which feels that personal wholeness involves the expansion of all the characteristics of the personality. A friend said to me, 'I feel I need to live out fully whatever is possible in my life, and that inevitably seems to lead me into something which I call sin. If I explore all the possibilities that life offers me, then I am certainly going to do some things which I will wish I hadn't. Or I can live a very cautious, narrow, uncreative life, and not risk anything. It seems to me that living fully means taking the risk that sometimes I may get it wrong; but I'd rather live like that – though certainly I sense that if I live fully, I am going to need forgiving.' Well, we all need forgiving, whether we live fully and get it wrong or whether we avoid that risk and betray our livingness. There is a constant need to discriminate between an expansion simply of the personality and the greater wholeness which justifies disobedience. But at the other end of the spectrum of temperament is the person who senses the path of righteousness underfoot and holds to that awareness, seeming thus to be less liable to sin, but who risks a spiritual narrowness and a lack of generosity towards others.

Perhaps the inevitable accompaniment to this path is a sense of failure, rather than guilt. If we truly are trying to be part of the whole pattern of grace, what we do may not often deserve the name of sin in the earlier sense of disobedience, but it will very often be failure. We will fail the God we try to embody, fail other people who need us to find the new right thing to do, fail in honesty or fidelity or perseverance, fail our own growing vision. And as long as we are also under pressure from the standards of our community (and that may well be most of our life!) guilt towards the old way will be added to failure in the new, and the conflict between them will also be a source of failure. There is the possibility all the time of making mistakes, of doing things the wrong way, of losing a closeness to God; but I think that there is less possibility of breaking oneself away from him. When our vision is of the spirit within the law, and our need is for the Spirit's creative wholeness, we may often stumble but we are less likely to turn off the 'paths of righteousness'.

The new ethic also brings a new community and a new sort of healing. When the law and the experts in the law can no longer direct us through strange countries, we must turn to other explorers for guidance on the way. I would never suggest that we rely upon nothing but our own consciences; our perception and understanding always need to be checked. But there is no longer a hierarchy – the priest, and Christ, and God, in an utterly reliable vertical line. Support and instruction come now from being part of a network, a wide, loose community all trying more or less well, all failing some of the time, and all able to care for the others in the mutual task. Lev Gillett offers wholesome advice:

> There are very definite criteria to judge guidance. First of all a guidance should not come only once; it must be repeated. Secondly, it must be spoken with the style of God; that is very important. God has his own language, his own style . . . Thirdly, you may test a guidance by sharing this guidance with other people. Ask four or five people who understand your problem to pray for a solution and to ask for guidance, and see whether the answers are convergent. Fourthly, the most definitive: does this guidance create in you sorrow, bitterness, hatred? Or does it create in you joy and love for God and for other people? Judge the tree according to its fruit.[13]

The fruits of the spirit remain the same; but perhaps now they ripen in a different way.

If, as I believe, there is a change as more people are being challenged to make creative ethical choices, and if it is developing a new definition of sin and an ability to accept failure, then there will also be a different sort of forgiveness and absolution. When a person's choice is for the ethic of creativity and therefore is implicitly or openly against the collective, the forgiveness of the collective – expressed historically in confession and absolution within the church – will not be available, but that person's self-forgiveness will often not be strong enough to support him or her in the painful situation. Many people, therefore, find their forgiveness now in small self-help or therapeutic groups, and from honest but loving friends, or they learn a more effective way to forgive themselves if they risk the exposures of psychotherapy. When we know that other individuals will share with us their own exploration and will try to understand ours, when we can believe that they will not think in terms of 'guilty' or 'sinful' at all but will want to find and share wholeness, then we can trust them in a completely different way. Our absolution will come from other travellers in mutual healing; horizontally through our neighbour, so to speak, rather than vertically through ecclesiastical authorities.

## Exploration is evolution

I believe that ours is a time of such widespread and turbulent change that it will amount to an evolution in culture and consciousness. I believe that what each of us does, so haltingly and uncertainly, about our values and ideals and our fears and needs contributes to that qualitative change. Sin and guilt and failure and weakness are germinating places for the spirit, when they are consciously faced and the truth sought beyond them. William Eckhardt says that truth has different meanings according to different levels of development. 'At the compulsive level, the truth is whatever theory serves the purpose of power, that is, the power of the few to determine the lives and surroundings of the many.' At the conformist level, it is 'whatever theory serves the purpose of maintaining the status quo, law, and order'. At the compassionate level, he says, the truth is what 'serves the purpose of changing minds and societies in the direction of compassion'.[14] We have to choose our truth; and I in writing this book and you in reading it must start that choice with our choices about sin and guilt. Eckhardt argues for compassion, which is a very personal value; similarly, I argue for personal choice and change, rather than the collective *status quo*.

We have to ask, 'How much of what is called my sin is so by somebody else's standards? What are my standards?' And if the answer is that by our own standards this is indeed sin, then we have to question, 'Can those other people give me the guidance I need now in this situation?' If they can, or might, we would be foolish not to turn to them; but if the answer is no, then the time has come to decide on our own values and make our own choices from them.

There is always a tension between obedience and creativity – and there should be. A condition of total creativity would be chaos; creativity must work upon something, and in this field its material is the existing situation, the collective mores, the individual as he or she is. Tradition and the weight of inertia in most of the population serve as a counterbalance to chaotic change, as well as a constant goad to creative effort from those who cannot conform. The collective has always been seen as being right, and disobedience was defined exactly as disobeying the collective and its leaders; but creativity necessarily involves disobedience, breaking and changing the rules, making something that the rules did not allow for. Both the collective – in the sense of our society, community or family – and we ourselves must accept this tension and see that it is a fruitful one, even when the strains, both individually and in social structures, seem nearly intolerable.

Therefore we have a new responsibility, no longer to the collective and its standards and its survival, but to something unknown which is growing around and within us, sensed but not yet seen. Even, perhaps, to making a *new sort of collective*, a more flexible, more equal, much wider community of shared and respected values as the basis for differing but co-operative standards.

The ancient Jews honoured that which is right, and believed that when a man sinned he could return to the 'paths of righteousness' by his own efforts to obey the Law. Then Jesus taught that it was the spirit not the law which would set us free; but over the centuries not only was a new law codified for us but we were warned that the *only* right path was the one marked out by the authorities, and we became doubly unfree. Now is a time to return again to the guidance of the spirit. I have been describing a new righteousness and new ways to travel. They are no longer those of the law, but they are not a lawless anarchy; they are born of humble personal responsibility. Our own individual efforts are necessary if the wholeness and rightness of the spirit is to grow in the world; we are responsible for our own decisions about what is right and wrong, for accepting forgiveness and using it, and for bringing vision into actuality. In our daily lives, we are now responsible for looking at all issues of sin and guilt in the light of the two ethics. We may then choose obedience, but it will be a conscious true choice, not by default; we may choose creative exploration, but it will include respect for those who honestly follow a known but not easy pilgrims' path.

Dearly beloved Friends, these things we do not lay upon

you as a rule or form to walk by, but that all, with the measure of light which is pure and holy, may be guided; and so in the light walking and abiding, these may be fulfilled in the Spirit, not from the letter, for the letter killeth, but the Spirit giveth life.[15]

## Naming the shrines

Thus, by these routes we come to the new and unknown holy places. Each shrine will be unknown while we travel, and recognized only when we reach it.

It is the sense of guilt which cuts off the God within. By the values we have been developing on our exploration, the retention of guilt and the failure to forgive oneself are primary sins! We have promised to travel, and guilt would keep us stationary. One of the first of the shrines, therefore, is self-forgiveness.

Sin, we agreed, is an avoidable and deliberate act which damages livingness; but there is a deeper sin (or rather, state of sin) which is an almost deliberate act of unawareness. It is a choice not to be aware of damage; conversely, we discover now that just being aware is a holy place. Even the awareness of our failure is not a dark place, because its context is the wholeness and rightness which is so sweet to us.

Humility is more than a shrine; it is a great open space. It is that dual vision, on the one side of the splendid wholeness of God, immeasurably greater than we are, enduring and vibrantly alive beyond any harm that we can do but lovingly eager for our coming, and on the other side, of the modest but unique and creative contribution to the wholeness which we each make in our travelling.

We are blessed also every time we have the chance to share with another traveller. When neither of us is burdened by guilt and both of us are tender towards failure, when there are no hidden comparisons of goodness but instead the hopeful exchange of understanding, then it is as though we had bivouacked for the night in a holy place.

Much of the time we will feel groping, lost and fearful. It is all new country, and hard travelling. But time and again we will know that we are explorers because we touch new shrines.

# 3

## THE WOMB OF THE SPIRIT

**The earliest care, the oldest hurts**

A pilgrim or explorer may be hurt at many different times in life, and may be hindered in the family setting, or by cultural or ecclesiastical pressures. But I want to concentrate on the earliest wounds, those which are most hidden in us and yet which are the ones we most need to uncover if we are to know ourselves. This is where the foundation of our lives can be flawed, so that we find ourselves, years later, 'doing that which we would not, and hating that which we do'.[1] The personality characteristics which have their beginnings in these earliest experiences and reactions will grow into crushing guilts, fixed attitudes of sin, or repeated falls however good our intentions.

During the long slog of my own effort to understand myself, I found the most help from a particular way of looking at infancy. In this model (see 'Further Reading'), a baby goes through various stages of vulnerability and of developing strengths during the early months, so that it responds to strains and difficulties in different ways according not only to its inherent temperament but also to the stage its young ego has reached when they happen. I use 'ego' in a very specific sense, as the executive centre of the personality, perceiving outer and inner events, handling information, making choices, responding and acting. It is a part of ourselves which at the beginning is individual but unformed, open to every influence like an egg without a shell, and which we develop into a functioning centre through our own particular interaction with other people and the world. I distinguish the ego from other, deeper parts of ourselves; but I will come back to that in a later chapter.

In the first nine months or so after birth, the baby is still in 'the womb of the spirit'.[2] Just as its body grew in its mother's physical womb, so its personality and spirit is formed within the first very special intimacy with her (or another person who provides the regular intimate care), until the spirit can 'gradually be born to an awareness of its now separable self-hood . . . From the beginning, the baby comes into being as a person, gains self-hood and the sense of identity, by responding to the light of the mother's countenance.'[3] If a baby has responded to the delight and acceptance it sees in its mother's face, it can then go on to discover the world beyond her with confident curiosity. Clearly, a baby does exist separately from the mother, but it only slowly develops an awareness of itself as separate from her, with its own world of which she is a major part but only a part, and its own responses and feelings which are often different from hers. If it experiences care and well-being throughout its earliest dependence, it will have the secure beginning of a sense of its own being, and in later life of an ability to believe in and identify with Being-itself. Its ego can become competent and assured, so that within its personality the spirit and the deeper self can develop and flower. But this impressionable openness to influences from its intimate world also make a baby deeply vulnerable to any failure, hurt or rejection which that world brings to him or her. It cannot negotiate or escape, cannot protect itself, cannot *understand*. Whatever happens to it, the bad and damaging as much as the good and nurturing, gets right through to its centre.

I do not want to suggest that a baby needs a perfect mother in order to develop a competent ego, and I appreciate Winnicott's reassuring phrase 'good-enough mothering'; but there is no doubt in my mind that the quality of the earliest care really is crucial. The lives of numberless people demonstrate that the lack of it can be overcome in later years, but this is done with tremendous pain and difficulty. What a responsibility this is for parents, and especially the mother as the one who usually gives the primary care; and, in our climate of increasing psychodynamic interpretation, it is a responsibility which often becomes a burden of undeserved guilt. A baby will experience its mother's illness, or its own, as a terrible deprivation or an inflicted harm, yet who could prevent or undo the event? To the infant, inescapable separations are desertion, and weaning difficulties can be experienced as cruel punishment; and the parents may be unable to understand or helpless to prevent the trauma, so that the wounds are deep and unhealing.

These oldest, deepest hurts are the hardest to uncover and understand. In the first months the foundations of our personalities are laid, and the ways we manage then to cope or endure, or to resist or run away, all contribute later to the pressures towards specific wrong-doing. Most of our inauthentic guilt, also, has its roots in these earliest reactions. Even many of our ideas of the nature of God, and the attitudes which separate us from him, are inevitably formed by our early experiences in relationship. Sometimes these views may seem to others to be very distorted (though they can usually be supported by some group or other, some theology or school!) and they can cause us much anguish; and sometimes we have to struggle with them as much as with the guilts and sins which are tangled up with them.

I do not believe that we are born evil, not even born tainted, but our temperaments and our painful experiences combine to make us vulnerable to sin and inclined to particular sins. We need to understand the pains we have suffered in order to deal most effectively with the sins we are tempted to commit. We are 'compelled to scrutinize the deepest, darkest, and most fearful parts of ourselves, the parts we all strive to deny or not-see. The thoughts which are most difficult to grasp or express are those which touch on this forbidden region and re-awaken in us our strongest denials and our most profound intuitions.'[4]

## Acceptance and being

According to this way of looking at infancy, the first phase of our lives is that of **acceptance**, when the sense of inner *being* starts. This is the time when the baby absorbs its mother's delight, responding instinctively to her welcoming smile; when it experiences total security as her supporting arms enclose it through every fear; when the only world it knows, the warm mother, comes to it in reassurance, whatever the need. This is the time when the core of the personality is formed, and if all goes well the individual can grow up, even through great difficulties, with something unbreakable at that centre. But if the baby does not feel completely accepted during this vulnerable time, there is not yet any development of an effective ego-structure which can handle wounding pressures. Mothers often fail their babies; most of it is unwitting and unwilled, although too much is the result of the mother's own hidden pains reverberating in her present actions. There are also many hurtful events which no one could have prevented, illnesses or family troubles, accidents and social pressures, which the baby suffers either directly or because the family is suffering them. But a tiny baby does not know anything about explanations and justifications, it just experiences totally whatever actually happens to it. If that is harmful, frightening or isolating, then a baby feels it as raw privation, the complete absence of good, and its whole being suffers the consequences. It suffers *non-being*. I think that it is almost impossible to over-emphasize the importance of this danger. As William Eckhardt says,

> the self-esteem of the very young child (not to mention his very survival) is determined by older persons in his environment. If they fail to feed him properly, he will become physically sick and he may die. If they fail to love him properly, he will become mentally ill and he may despair, contracting a 'sickness unto death' which is not physical.[5]

A baby only a few weeks old has no sense of time or space. If a mother delays her coming for only five minutes, it has no way of knowing that there will be a sixth in which she may appear; if she is only in the next room, she does not exist for it. When the baby is asleep or peaceful that does not matter, because the whole world is asleep or peaceful; but when it is hungry, frightened, or in discomfort, its whole world is one of distress, which quickly grows into threatening anguish. The only way for a baby to handle severe distress at this early stage, whether it is sudden and acute or milder but constantly repeated, is by a very primitive psychological mechanism called 'splitting-off'. The unbearable pain has to be cut off from the dawning consciousness, so that the baby can find ways to relate and respond again. 'What cannot be borne is denied',[6] but it remains buried in unconsciousness as an unending terror that the agony will recur. After that, the denial must be continued, permanently; the memory and its emotions are intolerable and they must never be allowed to return to consciousness, so they are 'repressed'. This word is often used loosely for something which is pushed out of the mind and denied attention; but it really means something which never comes into the mind at all, because it is forcibly and continuously hidden from consciousness.

The most important thing for a baby is that its mother should come when she is wanted and needed. Once held by her, it can wait a considerable time for food or physical comfort; but it cannot wait for her coming. In the empty world of the child who craves response, all time is forever and all experience absolute. Therefore, if a baby is left alone for longer than it can bear, its first reaction is unimaginably intense fear of being deserted. If the pain remains just within what it can tolerate, so that it can continue to long for the mother who will end the terror, the ground is prepared for the later development of a fearfully clinging personality. Clearly, a single or even an occasional harsh experience will not determine the personality, because babies, like humans of all ages, are marvellously resilient, and a lot of loving for the rest of the time may greatly lessen the effects of a traumatic experience; but there will inevitably have been some degree of shaping influence. If what happens is actually the loss of the mother, through death or very long absence, then the baby not only suffers the terror and anguish, but also has good reason to fear desertion again.

Therefore, a clinging personality in adulthood is the outcome of a long defence against re-experiencing that early terror. (On the whole, it is more likely to be found among women, so I will use just 'she' for a while.) As the child grows older, and then into adulthood, the continuing anguish is repressed, but the necessity for protection against it remains strong, so this person always needs someone to belong to, is always fearing desertion, and unable to endure the emptiness of solitude. She hangs on to attachment of any quality because isolation threatens to sweep her away into non-being. She will pursue a lost lover or husband with tears and pleading; every new acquaintance becomes the possibility of 'real love at last'; grown-up children are badgered for attention – because for her, love is never reliable or convincing. She *needs* people, to care for, to depend upon, to interact with; and her main attitude in trouble is likely to be frightened and pleading, though she may make many, and pathetic, attempts to hide her weakness and to 'cope'. She has a constant struggle to avoid seeing the inner threat of non-being, the panic feelings and overwhelming anxiety; indeed, she has to keep all this fear out of consciousness, if possible. A person like this is not basically angry, though anger may flash out in fearfulness or frustration. Instead, trouble or crisis stirs up a vague dread which she cannot even describe convincingly. The poor sufferer may not often recognize this as mental pain because she will have so many neurotic ways of hiding it from herself, or will concentrate just on the physical symptoms of stress or illness, so that she does not have to face her fear.

Although no individual is a 'type', people nevertheless do incline towards certain reactions and behaviour. This sort of person will tend to particular weaknesses and failings, and if she is unscrupulous or not self-controlled, towards the wrong-doings and sins which arise from them. She is likely to be self-centred and selfish, perhaps oblivious to other people's feelings or, if she is aware, then certainly judging them less important than her own. What was the baby's dependence upon the mother's physical presence develops into an adult dependence upon the senses, upon seeing and touching what is needed and who is needed; but this simple enjoyment of the senses can easily grow into a damaging indulgence in them. Her sins are also likely to be those of clinging and demanding; she is usually angling for attention, and dislikes not getting it; she can be emotionally manipulative, with intense attachments and unreasonable rejections.

What matters in our context of the struggle against wrongdoing and sin is the way in which the later life of faith will also be influenced by such early loss or harm. This person's perception is likely to be of a God who 'absconds', who will not give care unless he is badgered by prayer and bribed and pleaded with, who comes and goes arbitrarily and will not stay. 'You cannot trust him, you can only try to trust him, against painful inner evidence to the contrary.'[7] What this poor woman needs most of all is the courage to face aloneness, which Paul Tillich called the 'courage to be as oneself'. It is a tremendous challenge to be oneself without anyone else who can be used to serve as a prop, or a confirmation.

I have described this personality type first partly because it is one I know very well. It was my own for a long time, and I was saved from the worst of it only by a very fierce determination to keep the strains to myself and not load them onto other people. Goodness knows where that came from – I like to think that it was grace. That was a decision which probably made my path more painful, even more difficult, but it lessened the struggle with the faults and wrongdoings which my sort of person has to resist. I have also been able to describe this type and its origins with confidence, because I have so often experienced the links between my feelings and fears and the childhood experiences which caused them. I am familiar with the road which must be taken out of desertion. In my life, I started from the actual implausibility of trust, and moved through total risk to a strange new form of trust which I could not have previously conceived because it exists alongside risk, all the time. I hope that some day I will even grow into unqualified trust.

I am surprised that cowardice is not listed as one of the seven deadly sins. It is certainly serious, for an incapacitating fear of harm or failure is nothing else than a lack of trust in God, though it masquerades as inability to trust ourselves or other people. Perhaps the neglect of this separating – when not positively sinful — attitude stems from the same avoidance remarked upon by a psychoanalyst whom I deeply respect. In a major study of fear, weakness and flight, Harry Guntrip comments on the innumerable studies of anger and aggression compared with the dearth of material about fear:

> Unless we allow for a universal resistance to the proper recognition of our basic fear and weakness, it is hard to explain why an 'instinct of aggression' has been given such prominence in psychoanalytic theory, while the equally obvious phenomena of 'instinctive fear and flight' have been so passed over.[8]

It seems that even therapists prefer to deal with the big, bad characteristics rather than the weak and wobbly ones!

More recently, in an excellent essay on a feminine view of the human situation, Valerie Saiving criticizes contemporary theology for identifying sin with self-assertion, pride, and will-power. The specifically feminine forms of sin, she says,

> are better suggested by such items as triviality, distractibility, and diffuseness; lack of an organising center or focus; dependence on others for one's own self-definition; tolerance at the expense of standards of excellence; inability to respect the boundaries of privacy; sentimentality, gossipy sociability, and mistrust of reason — in short, underdevelopment or negation of the self.[9]

These faults may be specifically, but they are not exclusively, feminine. They are the weaknesses, and can lead to the sins, of anyone with a clinging need and the over-compliance of fear, whether a woman or a man.

## The wound of non-being

If the terror of the mother's absence continues so long that it overcomes even clinging neediness with its underlying fear of abandonment, then the infant psyche explodes inwards, so to speak. Need and longing are natural in a baby, even when they become terrifyingly exaggerated, but there has to be a backlash from a need which has become shattering, which lasts so long that there is no more emotional energy to sustain it. When the tiny personality is unable to endure any more it escapes, totally and from everything. The baby simply repudiates all its longing for the acceptance and care which would not come to it, and the result is a radical and enduring withdrawal which is basically very unnatural. What then develops is an almost complete inability to relate, sometimes a rejection of relationship, and inability even to try to trust. When the mother does at last return, when her care does come to the child, it does not help – it has come too late. It is as though care or not-care no longer matter; a self which has withdrawn so far to escape not-care has gone too far to feel care either. But this core of the self is now in nothingness; identification with *non-being* has happened, and the hidden self is overwhelmed by a constant, nameless dread.

Through all of childhood, youth and adulthood, this suffering person cannot find any centre, any self; he is a 'hollow man' – and the greater number of this type do seem to be men, though often some degree of this condition underlies the fearful weakness we have just looked at, adding an extra urgency to the clinging which tries to keep it at bay. But one cannot live in non-being and nothingness without going mad, so his whole life is an exhausting struggle to repress all the pain and fear, and to maintain an appearance of being. Since emotion is a minefield, he may rely upon his intellect alone to provide that, and his relationships may always have a strangely detached or ethereal quality, and an absence of commitment. He is cool and distant, disliking emotional intimacy, distrustful and uneasy. In his religious life, he may always have difficulty in experiencing any feeling of belief and of God, and will instead have to depend upon intellectual conviction. He may seem to be guilty of unbelief, that is of an actual refusal to believe, but indeed he cannot believe that there is a good or loving God, for he has not any radical experience of the very first goodness which would make that believable.

He may also carry the burden of constant apathy and futility, for without the vitality of central being all life and effort seem worthless. This is a characteristic which other people find inexplicable and frightening, and its persistence can further burden him with guilt towards them and hopelessness about himself. The defences against such an agonizing state have to be rigid and very strong, so they are also energy draining, and when a person like this breaks down in depression, it lacks the agitation and anger of simple, or classic, depression and has a particularly crushing and deathly quality.

It is difficult for me to think in terms of sin or guilt at all, about a person with wounds this deep, because so much of what he does – or she, because there certainly are women who suffer such anguish – will be built upon a helpless reaction to literally intolerable pain. Sometimes what seems like guilt in them turns out, upon closer and sympathetic examination, to be instead a permanent expectation of punishment though there is no knowledge or sense of wrongdoing. But, to the extent of his adult responsibility for his actions and the harm they cause, the wrong he does must be called sin, and his sins will be mainly those of isolation. The person will often, and perhaps always, cut other people off, and may therefore seem unloving, and will certainly not easily or adequately communicate love; so the primary characteristic of sin – damage to livingness – will always be a possibility. Even though it is especially important for a person like this to help others to understand his or her involuntary isolation, it is difficult even to recognize it in oneself, because the wound is so hidden, and trying to uncover it is so agonizing. He will retire into a rigid emotional cowardice, refuse to face that most inward despair, and be consumed by hatred of his own weak core personality. But his retreat will not show; keeping up a superior front will be essential. His isolation and the need to construct a substitute for real self-esteem will be likely to lead to that unpleasant sort of pride which belittles others. He will also be prone to the failing, which can become the sin, of rejecting his own livingness. Frank Lake calls it a 'self-centred and morbid withdrawal from life'. Why should he want life when it is so painful? It does seem difficult to place this one among the classic sins, and yet how much harm it can cause.

This sufferer is likely to think of God in terms of the early devastating dependence, as the one who inflicts anguish and terror. The thought of him threatens punishment and pain; it is hard to believe that he might ever bring love or kindness or forgiveness. This is a God who created a universe of evil and suffering, and seems to care little for the creatures in it. A God who needs to be forgiven. If the individual belongs to a church, he will probably try to suppress this view; but any other will either seem unconvincing to him, and hypocritically held, or will be held desperately and perhaps fanatically in an attempt to convince himself. He had no foundation in infancy for faith, if faith is considered to be a strong and willing trust, because there was no experience of trustworthiness. For this person more than anyone else, faith in adulthood must become a 'leap of faith', a choice to be always at risk, a perpetual living 'as if'.

Ordinarily, sinners need to be reconciled to God by forgiveness or the recognition of pre-existing forgiveness; but a sufferer from this degree of dereliction may find reconciliation only if he receives evidence that God shares his suffering. He needs something more than not being alone – he needs to realize that God too is in pain and is present and suffers with him, that the two of them are truly companions. He cannot be *blamed* for the condition which leads to his particular forms of sin, but he is nevertheless *responsible* for not harbouring them, and the most important step towards that is acceptance of the pain from which his sins provide a retreat. Frank Lake, whose *Clinical Theology* was for me the deepest and most compassionate enlightenment I found on this subject, expresses a Christian's view of this responsibility:

> This inner cross can be accepted or rejected by the adult just as decisively as a piece of purely contemporary persecution . . . There is no cross or persecution which leaves the adult so free as to whether he will or will not, for Christ's sake, bear it, as the pain of his own inheritance of repressed suffering . . . Is there not a richness of reconciliation in the Cross, not only for those whose inescapable problem is their culpable sin, but for those whose inescap-

able problem of faith or unbelief lies in their inability to be reconciled to the devastating evils which came upon them in their innocence?[10]

Traditional views of sin and guilt may be of so little help to such a wounded person as to seem irrelevant. But here if anywhere an individual and creative ethic can apply. The 'sinner' needs to recognize himself as a sufferer, has to admit he is a sufferer, helpless and vulnerable, has to take the enormous risk of asking others to understand him and to embrace his incapacity. Where the sin is so likely to be one of rejection of others, asking others for affirmation will seem like penance indeed! He needs to 'affirm his despair', which Kierkegaard says is the first act of faith; he needs the courage to admit his isolation and to risk participating in a community or a pair. This is what Tillich has called 'the courage to be as a part'. The first retreat was an attempt to escape annihilation, but it resulted in a frozen nothingness. All real contact reawakens that early terror of annihilation, but if it can be faced, and relationship – with people and with God – risked, then warmth and emotional movement become possible at last.

## Rage and substitutes

Both of the personality types we have just looked at arise when the helplessness of the infant is so great that resistance to mistreatment, or even to poor handling or misfortune, is impossible. But sometimes a baby with a particularly active and energetic temperament can manage to resist being overwhelmed by the terrors of neglect and desertion, even in the first weeks. If so, his vigorous energy feeds a shapeless rage, not against anything or anyone in particular, such as the mother personally, for so young a baby cannot really be aware of objects or people as separate from itself, but he simply fights against the state he is in, which is the threat of no longer existing. At the core of the baby, the power of being-itself is waning, but he hangs on to the situation furiously. It is threatening and frustrating beyond measure, but it is simply his whole universe, and he will not admit helplessness and defeat, and retreat from it. His seething or exploding rage is his proof of self-existence, even at that minute age. He may scream and kick and vomit (and, poor creature, thus sometimes invite more actively repressive treatment), or live out his rebellion in wordless but intense fantasies of combat and resistance.

Sometimes, also, the more clinging personality which we first examined may harbour a degree of rage which can be used to resist the primary dread. This works because to be angry at the mother, or at the situation of waiting for her, is to remain involved with her and therefore to deny her absence. When grown up, such a person is less likely to weep and plead with anyone who causes her anxiety and pain, but rather to accuse and punish. She is very likely to blame others for all the difficulties which arise, and instead of being simply, and often subterraneously, manipulative she may well resort to open emotional blackmail.

The second basic response of an active temperament is 'lust'. This is another one of those old-fashioned words which has become narrowed to just a sexual meaning, but one of my dictionaries calls it a strong desire to possess and enjoy, and an older one says 'irregular, inordinate or unlawful desire'. It is not just sexual greed, but any craving which becomes an overriding preoccupation. Lake, as usual, puts across the essential, and compulsive, element: 'an absolute desire for that without which one cannot exist'.[11] The baby is denied the mother's loving presence, but with all its energy it staves off the time of total deprivation by fantasizing the comfort and satisfaction which it craves. Active, compulsive fantasy may then become a permanent part of the personality, whatever the object – food, beauty, success or sex. The power of being-in-relatedness diminishes whenever there is trouble or failure, but there is always the fantasy of a substitute, grabbed for with desperation because the need is absolute and essential, and repeatedly because the need can never be filled. This may not in itself be active wrongdoing, though it certainly lessens the reality and effectiveness of life, but the lust for substitutes rarely remains just fantasy in adult life, and is a potent breeding ground for many sins.

## Well-being in sustenance, fury in loss

A baby who feels fully accepted in the first months of life, because its central being is confirmed by the mother's presence and delight, can move on into the phase of **sustenance** with confident trust in *well-being*. It expects discomfort to be attended to and is not disappointed, it expects and receives all the food it needs, and its growing abilities are welcomed and encouraged by its loving family. It becomes confident that the world and the people in it are reliable and benevolent. 'The quality of well-being, good spirits, courage and personal vitality is a reflection of what has been communicated from others in this [earliest phase of life].'[12] If the baby has had a bad start, there may always be some hidden weakness in the personality which trouble in later years could uncover; but loving care through these months will do a lot to heal any earliest damage. This is the period when the ego first begins to form, still as tentative and uncertain as the wavering hands which reach out for a toy and only sometimes grasp it, but already individual and very capable of learning. Its characteristic responses are beginning to develop, the ability to wait increases, the passivity and fear which marked the earlier helplessness give way to demand and complaint.

But the very existence of a developing ego-structure gives the baby the strength to rebel against pain or deprivation which happen at this stage. Difficulties – such as those which centre upon sudden or troubled weaning – are not an absence of what is vitally needed but are an active taking away of a good which has been expected and enjoyed. A baby with an energetic temperament is likely to respond with fury; not the inchoate early rage (though perhaps building upon that) but a very positive and directed rebellion against the loss of what was his by right. The little ego has some strength now to resist a fall into emptiness, and the baby will rage against what seems to be a harsh and depriving mother. We all know what it is like to go over and over a nasty scene in our minds, imagining what we would have said and done if we had had the chance, imagining a second encounter when we can get it all off our chests; it is no different for tiny children, though they have not any words and their emotions are wild and shapeless. So in this situation, a baby is gripped by wordless fantasies of punishment and retaliation, perhaps openly expressing them as temper, or perhaps inwardly suffering their disruption of his young personality although they are kept hidden from his consciousness.

Getting back at the world is the basic active response to deprivation. A person who suffered early experiences like this will be likely to hit out against criticism, retaliate against all slights and setbacks, will blame others for everything that goes wrong and always find excuses for himself. He may challenge and bully anyone weaker than himself or, conversely, disguise most of these characteristics with a false helplessness used as an excuse for all failure and to hide the way that failure actually succeeds in depriving others of the good which they need. His angry attacks can always be justified by the psychological mechanism of 'projection' in which an individual's hidden and denied emotions are unconsciously cast upon others, and seem to be their attitudes, not one's own.

It is so important for us to realize that a baby cannot be considered guilty of the rage, recoil or manipulation with which it reacts to such terrors and pain. A barely-formed ego has only a few inadequate methods for dealing with damage, and it uses them blindly. Unfortunately these feelings can lead to such a sense of fundamental personal badness that it can hardly be distinguished from guilt in later years. Alice Miller says that 'every patient clings to fantasies in which he sees himself in the active role so as to escape the pain of being defenceless and helpless. To achieve this he will accept guilt feelings, although they bind him to neurosis.'[13] It is better to feel big and bad than small and weak. Because the origins of the guilt are hidden from consciousness, the desperate adult may persistently search for the causes of it, and endlessly refute the blame, in a resentful circuit of misery, guilt and self-justification, defensively alternating with retaliation or pre-emptive emotional strikes.

So, regrettably, the characteristic sins of these bad-tempered or sullen personalities are especially unlikable, and it is often difficult to feel sympathy for them. They are envious of others' well-being, and jealous; suspicious, vengeful and grudge-holding; bullying; touchy and blaming; self-excusing and dishonest. Their angry lust, in fantasy and actuality, attempts to restore the lost good things and frequently exploits other people, emotionally or materially, to obtain them; their constant suspicion undermines all offers of the help, friendship and love which they so badly need and may even ask for; and there are frequent scenes in which they must come out best, so that they can be convinced of their own strength to retaliate. Their undeserved sense of guilt is unfortunately entangled with a real, adult responsibility for their behaviour against others, and it makes their unfairness and exploitation particularly difficult for them to admit to. 'When we see no way out of frustration, we transform the world into a hateful place to justify our anger, rather than admit that we have chosen to respond to frustration with aggression.'[14] This distortion leads to a very active unreality which is in some ways more difficult to counteract than the passive inauthenticity of more helpless sufferers. Well-developed fury is the most 'successful' of the psychological strategies, because the distorted personality structure is so tightly locked that it rarely breaks down. The energetic defences are rarely broken into, either, and potentially transforming influences do not easily get through to the angry sufferer.

Such people need a particular sort of courage. The first deprivation was a humiliation, a denial of their right and worth, and their strongest defence has been an attacking pride. They need now to bow their necks, to admit the emptiness and shame of losing whatever was theirs by right, so that they can accept God's forgiveness for the destructive methods which they have developed to compensate for the deprivation. They must realize that the fault for much present trouble is in themselves, not in those around them; but this is a particularly subtle problem, for in fact the very first fault *was* in others. Such acceptance is even more difficult because they are likely to see God as a betrayer, cruel and inconstant in the same way as the earliest carers were. He brings people into the world only to deprive them of the joy and security of life, what he gives is empty of meaning, and at any moment he may inflict even worse ills.

His is a sour, scornful face. How can such people believe that God will forgive them their fury, and accept them as they really are? Yet to risk the self-exposure of true acceptance is their only salvation; they need 'the courage to accept acceptance'.

A different sort of personality develops if these active responses, which are natural in a child of several months, have been undermined by the passive endurance of earlier damage. If an already hurt baby suffers severe deprivation at this stage, especially of milk but also of care and response, or if there is a complete sudden change of care, or a medical emergency, it may then fall back into the previous terrified helplessness. Its need can produce such mental pain that the emerging personality recoils into the earlier, and only partly overcome, fear of relationship, because to want the good thing would only be to have it refused yet again. The baby (and, later on, the adult) will not dare to hit back. Even though it may feel that sustenance is its right and that the mother must be present somewhere, it has no ability to protest at deprivation.

Therefore, when reliable care has suddenly stopped but the baby dares not rage against the mother it needs for its very life, a very complex situation develops. The young personality is crushed in a stark choice: if rage cannot make furious and aggressive demands, separation and deprivation may reach deathly intensity; but if the rage and its murderous fantasies do come into the open, it may destroy the mother, and even the world. So the poor baby is torn between its terror of a separation so dreadful that it would be annihilated, and its identification with the guilt and ultimate blame which its fantasies cause. The resulting conflict may become a fixed part of the adult personality, the rage turning inwards in exhausting depression more despairing and less apathetic than that of passive total vulnerability, but just as crippling in its own way.

A suspicious and resentful but frightened adult personality is always resisting a self-condemnation which grows out of the fear that the early deprivation was actually deserved. Often in later life, if trouble like the loss of a job or the failure of a marriage undermines self-esteem and precarious well-being, this sort of person will withdraw from the unhelpful world, and become confusedly preoccupied with himself or herself, and lost in all the anxieties and difficulties. Such a person is lonely and in desperate need of acceptance, but cannot believe in any love, affection or help which are offered, and he or she even resents the well-being in others which has the strength to offer it.

A person with this hurt *and* angry past has to find many ways to cope with or to hide the conflict, and the failure to cope always threatens. Most aspects of life will seem unreliable, and God most of all. At times it is possible to believe in his warm acceptance, at others he will appear hard and rejecting; he gives well-being, then accuses and threatens. 'One thing is certain, he asks the impossible. One cannot trust him; one can only propitiate him. One can only make a good show in the hope that he will overlook all that you have swept under the carpet, of rage and lust.'[15] But he is so unreasonable and unjust that if one fails to propitiate him then damnation is a probability. Guilt and self-blame are constant, exasperation and even fury against oneself may be frequent. The only resource in this pitiful case is the courage of despair, admitting the conflict and its terror, and affirming the existence of value even when it cannot be experienced.

So, in the way of looking at infancy which has been most helpful to me, these are the earliest wounds, briefly described. Often they will have been involuntarily inflicted, because of ignorance, clumsiness or unfortunate circumstances, and the 'good-enough loving' which follows them will draw most of their poison. But some will remain, to contribute to the formation of the personality, and to cause the weaknesses which can lead to sin. And too often, in other cases, they do arise from what now is openly called 'child abuse', and will be deepened and intensified by continuing bad treatment. Alice Miller knows what happens to children who are hurt, humiliated, neglected or ignored:

> A loved child receives the gift of love and with it that of knowledge and innocence. It is a gift that will provide him

with orientation for his whole life. An injured child lacks everything because he lacks love. He doesn't know what love is, constantly confuses crime with good deeds and mendacity with truth, and hence will continue to be subject to new confusions.[16]

It must be clear that we cannot in any real sense be held responsible for our babyhood reactions and ways of surviving. As with knowledge about the survivors of adult torments, of concentration camps, wars and torture, we can only be humble before the ability to survive at all. A baby has so few choices, so little ability – it cannot be blamed for what little it manages. But as adults, now, needing and hoping for closeness to God, we do have a responsibility for looking into our hurt hearts and doing what we can to change and improve the way we reacted then and to some extent still do.

# 4

# MASKS, KNOTS AND BRUISES

## Status and masks

As a child comes up to a year old, it starts to build upon that first involuntary foundation; its young ego can just begin to take part in shaping its personality. It has developed some awareness of the passage of time, and can distinguish itself a little more clearly from whoever cares for it. True relationship between two persons now starts to take the place of the previous identification, when the boundaries between itself and its mother were slight and sporadic. If there has been a good beginning, it can remember how often she has responded in the past, and therefore is better able to endure delay and difficulty; we could say that it has developed a simple degree of faith. This is the period when **status** grows out of the previous **acceptance** and **sustenance** – status in the sense of finding one's place in the intimate community of the family, with a feeling of belonging and a consciousness of one's own ego. The child is beginning to develop what will be a true self-respect based upon having been valued and having received the care and attention which expressed that value. In healthy growth, it is a time of open-hearted confidence, of energy and enjoyment, and curiosity about people and the world. The child welcomes the timely slight distancing from its mother which starts now. It is the beginning of an independence which is safe because her protective care has been proven and she is never far away. The baby's tiny world is an exciting place in which he or she feels confident, and secure enough to venture.

But if the previous months did not go well, this healthy confidence is missing. The first pain and fear will have been locked away, along with the unacceptable reactions to them, but they all exert a hidden pressure on the infant personality. There is a sort of 'double-mindedness' which results from the pressure to carry this mental and emotional burden, and yet find ways to relate within the family. These children try to gain belongingness by pleasing the mother and others, but that can only be done if they pretend to be what they are not. They *are* hurt, rejected, frightened and very needy; they must *seem* to be responsive and appreciative, obedient and competent. For them, belonging is not a loving gift, just because they are there and are themselves, but is a reward for 'good' or 'proper' behaviour, which has to be earned by constant effort. A while ago I described the super-ego as the part of our minds which imitates, probably in distorted and exaggerated ways, all the instruction, criticism and blame we receive. In a hurt or frightened child, the pressure of the super-ego becomes dominant at this period, because the early fear or fury must never be allowed to show. All the wretched secrets must remain hidden. The child feels forced into behaviour which it believes or learns will win it a desirable place in the family affections. Acceptance must be bought, and sustenance is conditional upon doing the required things, or even being the required sort of person. Theologically, says Lake, 'this is to replace justification by faith in the gracious character of the mother by the onerous method of justification by works . . . so as to earn what had previously been a gift.'[1] In other words, God does not love just because he is loving, but he only approves, and even then only when we keep the rules. 'The mentality of the servant has replaced the direct spirituality of the son.'[2] Or the daughter.

In this falseness, the growing child maintains the original emergency methods of splitting-off and repression to conceal the initial withdrawal, rage, blame or lust. They are human reactions, really, just inadequate ways of coping, but they are also unacceptable, both to the child and the family, so an appearance of their opposites develops, to hide them. Those terrible wounds, eating away at our spirits like ulcers, are denied by the scar-tissue which we grow over them. We develop neurotic ego-ideals with personality characteristics which are basically inauthentic. Psychiatrists label them 'reaction pattern formations', but they seem to be us, so hard do we try to fool ourselves as much as others. These are the layers of personality which we grow up with, and try to make sense of.

There is, for example, a mask of confidence and calmness which is used to cover the primary wound of acute separation-anxiety and its terrors. This pseudo-confidence is bolstered by an unconscious avoidance of situations which would provoke anxiety. Then it becomes necessary to lie about the avoidances, with more or less convincing explanations of the necessity for them. The original desolation, for example, is hidden by clinging and attachment which are justified in adulthood by the need to 'keep the family together', or the importance of one's exhausting committee work, or a thousand similar claims.

The draining fear of the death of the spirit, or the self, cannot – truly, cannot – be admitted. It is denied by a compulsive need to prove that one is not afraid, that one can deal with anything that happens, some way or another. An outsider can see this mask slipping sometimes, as when a person who is clearly ill pretends there is nothing wrong rather than face the truth which will test his or her courage. The struggle against illness would expose the weakness of the will to live, and this cannot be allowed into consciousness, so it is denied by angry protestations of strength and ability. Such a person tries to seem strong all the time, is a 'coper', 'independent' and 'capable', and certainly will not admit to tiredness or anxiety. 'To rest, to give up hope in oneself, to give up trying, all arouse a neurotic sense of guilt.'[3] Despair and apathy at the core are denied by compulsive optimism and persistence on the surface, as the individual flogs himself into constant effort. He is afraid that to relax his pseudo-zeal would be to disintegrate, so he becomes a workaholic and perfectionist, either driving others along with him, or feeling justified in his superiority. This is an *iron* mask; no less would serve the purpose.

Feelings of worthlessness are a fearful burden. The sufferer contradicts them with compulsive striving to be needed or important, and by touchy disagreement with all criticism. If these denials were just bandages, protecting a person's pain but not seeming to be his own skin, they could be examined and changed; but it takes a long time and a lot of personal work to reach that stage of understanding. On top of the bandages people wrap clothes which hide even further the anguish at their hearts, because all these denials and the early, unacceptable reactions to being hurt must in their turn be disguised if the façade is to be preserved. Any strong wish for attention rouses guilt because the super-ego calls it histrionics or ostentation, and so it is camouflaged by excessive self-effacement. Prudery and bigotry, often bolstered by the standards of a sect or school, refute hidden lustful fantasies of satisfaction. Distrust of a basically bad universe is covered up by idealization of parents, and later of the group one belongs to, such as a church or political party, and to demonstrations of what seems to be 'trust' because it adheres to instruction and tradition. Rage and destructiveness may be hidden by a sort of *rubber* mask, a compliant personality which is submissive, over-obliging, and afraid of disagreement, with an excessive concern for others and inability to express anger. The same sort of compulsively obliging availability may cover up a longing to run away from a painful situation or a bad relationship.

## Convolutions

As if all these torturous retreats from authenticity and spontaneity were not enough, in some people even the disguises are disguised. 'It does not do to *know* that we need to defend against unacceptable inner experiences and emotions. That is to say, the very fact of having to defend against intolerable emotions and impulses . . . demands a special reaction pattern formation as a permanent feature of character.'[4] Obsessional personalities manage, though with rigid effort, to maintain more than camouflage – they wear armour. Inflexible, over-conscientious, needing a rigid orderliness, attempting an impossible perfectionism, they try to control every chink and change. 'The personality must be kept inwardly in chains, inhibited, crushed into passivity, not allowed to be spontaneous in any way, but only allowed a very limited, circumscribed form of activity.'[5] These people can be exclusive, rejecting, righteously jealous – in every way uncharitable; but their actions will all be self-justified and rarely acknowledged as sins. Once again the absence of true guilt can be seen as a constriction upon growth.

But however bad the repression and strain may be at the centre of the personality, an individual may hang on to the distorted inner situation because at least it is a way to control and suppress the even deeper starved and angry needs. I know so well the condition which Harry Guntrip describes in *Mental Pain and the Cure of Souls*:

> In that state of mind one can know no peace: relaxation is impossible, wearing tension and conflict in body and mind is kept going by a persisting inner vicious circle of frustration, aggravation, repression, more frustration, and so on. The situation within the personality and the strain engendered may, and often does, get worse as the years go by, leading to recurring nervous breakdowns. The personality has developed on the basis of an inherently self-frustrating pattern. Here is mental pain in its most chronic form and in all its grim, stark reality.[6]

Guntrip is writing as a psychotherapist, and therefore refers to recurring breakdowns; it is as true to say that the situation leads to recurring sins, especially of the exploiting, controlling, manipulative types. Such sins cannot be condoned, of course, and it is necessary to seek a healing, maturing way out of them; but an understanding and self-understanding view of them is equally important.

Unfortunately, not all the reasons for holding on to defences and pretences deserve compassion. With so much bottled-up misery, it is reasonable to wonder why people do not more often long, somewhere or sometimes, to break free. The answer too often lies in what they are getting out of it. The pain, fear and limitation are primary; but what are called the 'secondary gains' may be very satisfying, and are certainly desperately desired. Sexual conquest, dominance in the family, career advancement, the anxious attention which an invalid receives, the frightened obedience won by bullying – these may be sweet to a hurt or angry heart, and not willingly exchanged for a deeper authenticity.

This structure of many layers, this tangle of reactions and disguises, creates an impression of convolution and confusion. But in *Soul Making*, Alan Jones uses an early concept from the psychoanalyst Melanie Klein to provide a simple framework for understanding it. Klein suggested that we cope with life by using three basic strategies: movement towards, away from, or against other people. In the last chapter we looked at the malfunctioning forms of these, in seduction, withdrawal or aggressiveness. The hurt and needy infant grows into an adult who moves towards people by clinging, and seeking care from 'the most powerful person in a group or the most powerful "God" in the pantheon of religions'.[7] The radically damaged baby moves away from others by becoming emotionally withdrawn; the angry, deprived one grows into a person who moves against others in hostility and distrust. But, says Jones, 'these are the neurotic forms of three basic movements that are important to all of us: to give affection, to stand up for oneself, and to keep apart on certain occasions. These have their religious counterparts: the longing for intimacy, the desire to belong without being swallowed up, and the hope for a true identity in God.'[8] By looking at the way we distort or misuse the strategies, we can learn something about which approach would suit us best if it were followed more positively. Our sins can be a guide to our potential saving graces.

All the pretending and lying, to ourselves and to others, and the need for the psychological characteristics which support it, are the source of much actual wrongdoing, and the cause of most of our struggle. Here is the classic 'onion' of the personality, layer after layer of disguise, pretence and denial, each one with its own temptations and typical wrongdoings, their sum adding up to a confusing and exhausting inauthenticity. They are all attempts to buy love; and even when they seem to succeed, bought love brings no healing. One of the dangers of the ethic of obedience is the way it can disguise our attempts to buy acceptance and love. But only 'the truth shall make you free' – the truth about our reactions and denials, about our defences and attacks, the truth about our fears and wounds. This personal labyrinth is the first ground of our exploring.

## Untangling the knots

Unwinding the tangle of our reactions and denials, in the effort of self-knowledge, is the preparation for any true journey. The road itself will have to lead through the acknowledgement of our more unpleasant hidden reactions, and into the true pain and loss of our earliest difficult experiences, whatever their degree may be. Most often, I can promise you, the pain will not be unbearable for adult experience, as it was for the helpless child; but there will be times, I know, when it will be long and terrible, to be borne by God's strength in us for we cannot carry it by ourselves.

Many, if not most, of the writers and practitioners in the various fields of psychotherapy would call all these reactions and denials neurotic. I cannot quite agree. I think that since we all have them to some extent, the term 'neurotic' would have to be so general as to be useless, or we would have to say that everyone is neurotic, which would be meaningless. This is human nature, the internal 'human condition'. I think that the term 'neurotic' is useful when such personality characteristics are, or become, so rigid or extensive that the person's life is cramped, limited and distorted by them, or if they often frustrate his or her ability to choose something better. If the internal pressures do become so great that they constantly threaten to erupt, then, it is true, a neurotic degree of defences and manipulations is necessary to keep the lid down; and when driven blindly by the earliest terrors and pains, or trapped in the neurotic structures of defence, a person can hardly be said to have true freedom of will, or to be held accountable for the hurt which he or she causes in turn. But even in that case, we must be careful not to use 'neurotic' either as an excuse, or a cause of hopelessness. There is still the one primary responsibility to look at what happens and try to understand it, in the nakedness of prayer and in honesty of meditation upon our actions and intentions.

The same responsibility is even greater for everyone who is not in such a desperate strait. Most of us do have areas of freedom even within our damaged personalities, which we can nurture and expand. The distortions we have examined are at the very least the source of petty, persistent wrongdoings, avoidable if the shame and pain are grasped, but starving life of reality if they are allowed to continue. This is where we all have to start, with simple adherence to decent individual standards of personal honesty and good intention, so that we may develop the strength to face the vulnerability of becoming our authentic selves.

These chapters are not only about what we have suffered and what has been done to us, but also about our need for authenticity, reality and the awareness of our real selves. What a friend I have found in the 'diary' of Georges Bernanos' humble, unconfident, clear-sighted country priest, encouraging me in the struggle to be authentic, sternly warning about the dangers of pretence:

> I believe, in fact I am certain, that many men never give out the whole of themselves, their deepest truth. They live on the surface, and yet, so rich is the soil of humanity that even this thin outer layer is able to yield a kind of meagre harvest which gives the illusion of real living . . . Yet by that same inner life shall they be judged . . . Therefore when death has bereft them of all the artificial props with which society provides such people, they will find themselves as they really are, as they were without even knowing it – horrible undeveloped monsters, the stumps of men.[9]

That need for authenticity is the beginning of my own answer to 'Why bother?' Why bother to struggle against sin and guilt if our long effort so far has only wearied us? Why bother to face our shameful manipulations if they still serve a protective purpose? Why expose our vulnerability, or take up the anguish of life, or labour to carry our suffering even though we may never lessen it? These are questions which rise again and again, and this is the core of my answer: because God is Reality itself, and deep in every person is the unquenchable longing to live in reality, truth, honesty and generosity. Deeper than all hurt, and more enduring than all other need.

So we commit ourselves to self-knowledge, and we start by looking at that tangle of what we do and why. If we are fortunate, there will not be all that many knots in it; but we have to be ready to work at whatever there are. In the first place, how do we tell what is a knot? Is modesty a genuine quality or a reaction-formation: are you really needed or do you make people need you? How do you know whether such characteristics are real, or are acceptable façades? Ah well — the answers come through another set of questions. Does compliance bring an understanding of other people's positions and a sense of co-operation, or does it leave you anxious that you have not done enough? Do you feel vigorous enjoyment of being needed, or a jealous resentment if you are not? Is it easy enough for you to be either unnoticed or the centre of attention, depending upon the situation, or do you seethe when you are neglected or panic when you are conspicuous? Real qualities are flexible and fruitful; façades are cramping and not always reliable. The fruits of the spirit are much the same now as two thousand years ago: 'love, joy, peace, patience, kindness, goodness, faithfulness, gentleness and self-control'.[10] Especially joy. When all is said and done, are you glad about what you feel and do? Are others?

Unfortunately, the things which you are not glad about may fit into other people's tangles, and they themselves will not want you to give them up! You may have to move quietly through this first stage, teasing out the strands of the knots and doing your best to understand them as you go, because if the process does reveal differences and even conflicts with others close to you or in your community, you will probably want to keep the door open to eventual reconciliation with them. In my experience, one finds help with the work of self-understanding, from individuals here and there, or small groups with a similar purpose; but the disagreements and readjustments in existing relationships and allegiances are likely to be extensive. After all, if you are questioning and trying to change yourself, you are also questioning and needing to change at least parts of your relationships, and are therefore by implication questioning others and suggesting that changes may be needed in them also. No person or organization takes easily to that sort of challenge. (You will not take easily to it yourself!) On the other hand, it is worth accepting the challenge and risk of anything good and glad in yourself or which is offered to you. So many of our defences and manipulations are attempts to avoid risk and to keep things the same, because the hidden, hurt part of ourselves cannot imagine any change that would not be even worse than what we already endure. But genuine mistakes and failures, even when they are painful, can usually lead somewhere because they are part of the movement of growth, which opens up new chances all the time.

This is not a book about psychotherapy, or marriage counselling, or personal and professional development; it is basically about religious life. Of course every part of your life will be closely involved in any attempt to understand your sin and its guilt and to find a way out of that struggle, but the natural place to turn for help in religion and spirituality is a church. Unfortunately, the churches increasingly fail the troubled and sincere people who turn to them, and in too many cases are even a source of confusion or the cause of further pain.

## The church-shaped bruise

The churches of all persuasions and in all their branches have been *the* authorities on sin and personal wrongdoing, and have often claimed to be the only means of forgiveness and cleansing. Now, through rigidity, self-righteousness and timidity, they repeat the old formulas or experiment uneasily with new ideas, in either case failing to support or help individuals more honest and courageous than the institutions they belong to or approach. I remember reading, years ago, a book called *The Painful Pew*, and being very glad that I was not in it! The churches markedly fail to acknowledge and treat the hidden personal wounds, and in this failure they add to the sufferers' pain. They also add many strains of their own. Meditating upon the lust for power and authority demonstrated by the chief priests who accused Jesus, Brian Thorne writes:

> We see the insidious workings of the lust for power and the egocentric craving to retain personal power and to preserve the absolute authority of the ecclesiastical institution. That is why religion can be a most destructive force in the life of human souls: it lends itself to an unscrupulous authoritarianism which cannot bear the uniqueness of persons and which beneath a cloak of virtue seeks to destroy those who by their inner security threaten its domination.[11]

Here, as in so many aspects of life, it is the disguise and deceit which are so hard to penetrate and resist.

I am fortunate to have escaped harmful pressure from my early church. I became aware of the social hypocrisy involved in my being sent to Sunday School and church while my father never attended and my mother only occasionally. It was thought to be in some way vaguely 'good for us', I suppose, and was certainly 'the right thing to do'. My brother played hookey; I lacked the nerve to do the same, but I covered up for him, and my own attendance became increasingly meaningless in my teens. I knew that there was a depth of meaning in life, but my church did not help me to find it.

Although as an adult I continued, for quite some time, a search for some way to express what I wanted to be a growing Christianity, I would not agree to any exclusivity or institutional certainty. I learned eventually (and reluctantly, because it left me lonely) that, since Jesus Christ is said to be unique, as the Son of God, the Christian church is inherently an excluding organization. Oh, I remember hearing and reading attempts to deny this, but I also remember my feeling that the arguments were tying their own feet in knots! I listen now with sympathy to my friends in more institutional denominations who struggle with the conflict between honesty about personal experiences and the authority of their churches. So much faith and sincerity, so much pain and confusion, so many individuals corseted by instruction or exhausted by resistance. Beyond that, so many more people of faith and integrity to whom the churches are almost irrelevant; they take it for granted that their spiritual journey will have to be solitary and without support. The modern believer believes in the Spirit which is encountered on the path, but doubts 'belief systems', and statements by religious professionals. There are a great many faiths, many denominations, many theologies – so, is everyone in step but our Johnnie? Or are we all marching to humanly fallible and varying drums?

No, the traditional churches did not wound me, and I do not think that they really hindered me, though they certainly gave me no help when I most needed it. But others are not so fortunate. In *Soul Making: The Desert Way of Spirituality*, Alan Jones asks, 'How do we number those who have been hurt and brutalized literally "beyond belief" by certain *ways* of believing? Such things are hard to document, but there is scarcely one of us who had not encountered many a wounded believer who thinks that he or she is an unbeliever.'[12] That is a terrible indictment, but I think it is not a false one. A friend told me that she thought the real harm which her church had done was to convince people that if they turned away from it they were therefore turning away from God. Jones continues, 'It is no wonder that many religious people are deeply angry and resentful. To be sure, their true feelings are often covered by a veneer of "oughts", "shoulds" and "good manners". Resentment is a natural response to unrealistic and unreasonable demands made on people, as if they were finished and complete entities.'[13] He quotes Harry Williams, 'Why do people imagine that in order to have God you must also have all this kind of nonsense? It is because . . . religion is to a large extent what people do with their lunacy: their phobias, their will to power, their sexual frustrations.'[14]

There is a somewhat caustic but useful relief which comes from admitting the possibility of organized religious lunacy! Both the troubled church member and the apologetic non-churchgoer not only have a right to examine doctrine and practice in the light of their own personal experience, but I hold that they have some obligation to do so. Before we can give a true obedience – and that may well be the outcome of our examination – we must have made our own assessment of what we are to obey. That assessment will have to include a compassionate uncovering of our wounds, as well as our own and God's forgiveness for the distorted personalities we have formed around them, and also honest exposure of the damaging structures, both personal and social, we have built or conformed to. It will at the least make us into very different pilgrims; and for most people the pilgrimage will then probably turn into an exploration. The obedient believer within a church always has to examine the arrangements of his life, comparing them with the standard of that church; the wounded sinner makes the same examination of his life before he can assess his sin, but he may find that he also has to examine his church in the light of the values which his wounds uncover to him. Our search may reveal our lack of belief in what the churches teach, but it is the expression of our faith in the God we seek.

A monk recently told a friend of mine, 'Your suffering is because you flinch from God's love. Forget yourself. There is only one principal sin: refusing to open to God's love – though to do so is the hardest thing on earth. Other so-called sins are nearly always injuries.'[15]

I believe he is right. Most sins do indeed germinate in an injured heart; and in practical terms it does not matter, anyway, whether your acts and attitudes are freely chosen or are the defensive reaction to injury, because the remedy is the same in either case: open to God's love. Over time, the clarity of that love will expose any truly sinful element, and its merciful support will strengthen you to grow out of the wrong; or its forgiving tenderness will enable you to uncover and tend to the injury.

## With a little help . . .

It must be clear that with a psychologically damaged background to many sins, psychotherapy will often be a great help in wrestling against them. But formal psychotherapy is not often available, and we usually have to manage with what we can learn or gain from here and there, to make us more able to follow our spiritual path. Frank Lake writes about this struggle from a psychiatrist's and pastoral counsellor's viewpoint:

> The very idea that mental pain may be part of the birth pangs of the spirit has become almost foreign to medical practice. But no one who still reads the bible or the lives of the men of God can escape this evidence, that dreadful inner doubt, distress and darkness accompany almost every major spiritual crisis. Some people are taken through this dark valley in solitary dependence upon God alone, faithful even when he seems most to have absconded. In one sense it is always a journeying alone . . . Withdrawal for spiritual renewal involves a shaking of the foundations in so far as they are less than thoroughly sound. But when God has done the shaking and a man has consented to the disturbance of this deeper digging, he returns to the world with a new basis in God-centredness and empowering . . . A clinical theology prepares men to use mental misfortune like a friend, as an unexpected 'negative' way to God, which, doubling back on the usual affirmative route, still meets God in the end. It prepares us to do without all kinds of reassurances we commonly demand.[16]

When there is a real commitment to change, opportunities to learn and develop do occur. A new friend brings a different perspective to us; a familiar sort of quarrel with a parent or spouse takes an unexpected turn and we even more unexpectedly feel able to follow it up and to change the stale dynamics; we have the chance to confide in a wiser or more compassionate priest than we had met before; a timely period of counselling or psychotherapy gives us just the help we needed to take a major step into the future; we fall in with a group of seekers who confirm us in the way we have chosen. One way or another we make it, as people have done for centuries, 'with a little help from our friends'.

# 5

# PARADOXICAL WOUNDS

In the previous chapter we looked at some of the ways in which we may have been injured very early in our lives, so that we could begin to understand the weaknesses, temptations and guilts which result. But sin itself is also wounding. It does damage in two ways, first by isolating the sinner from God, from his or her deeper self, and from other people, and also by harming those who suffer from the sinful acts and draining the relationships within which they happen. Wrongdoing and sins, whether our own or others', require from us two sometimes complementary but often opposing attitudes. We must not accept our own sins nor allow any compromise with them, and yet we must understand and believe that they are not us, that our goodness longs for love and to be loving, and that it *will* reach the light. Towards the sins of others we have to be unequivocal, utterly refusing to take part in them and to let them harm us, whatever else we risk or lose thereby, but it is also necessary to foster within ourselves not just compassion for the person who sins but also a longing to be united with him or her, in the goodness which we *can* share.

## The 'seven deadlies'

The wounds themselves are paradoxical. If we consider the traditional seven deadly sins, we often see qualities which are in fact valuable and creative. As a rule, anger, pride, covetousness, envy, sloth, gluttony and lust are attitudes of sin which do great harm because they are *disordered passions* – 'A passion is, in this context, an unintegrated drive, an unconscious compulsion. The will has little or no power over it. "Passion" in this sense refers to the danger we are in when we refuse to allow things to come to consciousness, when we repress what we can see, when we avert our gaze and turn our eyes away.'[1] But if we do look at them, honestly but not fearfully, searching for the valid and valuable form of the energy within them, we see qualities which are essential for our wholeness.

Anger is clearly not always a sin; only misused anger is sinful. Anger is a valuable, even an essential, energy, and yet most people are afraid of it in themselves as well as in others, are guilty about it, and critical or self-critical when it appears. But anger at what is wrong in life, and at our own self-bondage, can be liberating. Where would we be without the anger which challenges the sin being committed against us; which gives us, for example, the adult strength to say at last, about childhood injuries, 'What they did to me was wrong'; or which sustains us in a long resistance to social injustice? We need the energy of justified anger for our survival and growth. There is also a true and balancing anger to be drawn upon, for example, by the self-distrusting and conforming person who allows others to mould his or her life. It leads towards a recognition of one's own worth, and therefore a more realistic assessment of what one owes to other people and what is deserved by oneself, as a person; and it helps with the weighing of guilt at implied or imputed neglect and selfishness.

Anger is necessary for the 'prophetic interference' required to change one's life.

> The prophet in us says, 'NO! This is not the way the Creator wanted the universe to respond to the blessing that creation is. We can – we must – do things differently.' . . . The prophet knows something about trusting anger, trusting one's moral outrage, trusting what is intolerable. And moulding that anger and outrage into creative possibilities.[2]

Those who have started their lives in furious retaliation against harm need to cleanse and redirect their anger into useful channels; those who have chosen timorous compliance as a mode of relating have to risk anger and learn to use it. '[Saint] Paul's prophetic call, like every Christian's and ultimately every person's, is a call to transform the world from slavery and bondage to freedom and justice.'[3] This includes transforming our inner worlds, and for that we need an assertive energy which feels very much like anger but has a different goal. 'The prophet in us calls forth the excellence and beauty in each of us, it calls forth the best that we can give.'[4]

Alan Jones writes about the value of being angry with God, and quotes from the Jewish Hasidic tradition:

> I know there are questions that have no answers; there is a suffering that has no name; there is injustice in God's creation – and there are reasons enough for man to explode with rage. I know there are reasons for you to be angry. Good. Let us be angry. Together.[5]

Perhaps the important thing is to be 'together' – together with God, with one's true self, with another person, with a group. When alone we tend to be afraid of where our anger will lead us, and not least because if it is truly followed it will often take us into our pain. We are afraid of the shattering consequences of that. If we are angry in the company of another, especially if we are supported by prayer and honesty, we may be more able to press into and through it. For it is important that we *be angry*. If we hang back from its fullness, and merely whine or rant, we will not *break through* into the more creative part of ourselves beyond it.

Pride and anger are closely connected. Pride is rightly seen as the greatest of all the sinful attitudes, when the ego sets itself against the order of grace and the will of God. Pride justifies rancour and retaliation, and feeds on lies; it is enormously destructive. But the proliferating superstructure of pride indicates the need to keep hidden, especially from the individual himself, a core of unbearable self-contempt. Pride which is a compensation for weakness, which covers a hollow centre or disguises rage against being deprived or denies the humiliation of rejection, has to be rigid and exaggerated because it has no foundation in real self-respect. What such a person needs is exactly that wondering and grateful pride of being loved by God, and being wanted by others for what he or she truly is. Like any symptom of disorder, exaggerated pride is useful when its activity indicates to us the presence of a wound, and gives us the chance to look more honestly at whatever is beneath it. To do that we must remove the bandages, and we will feel very raw and exposed indeed. I doubt that any sinful attitude thrashes and squirms its way back into position more vigorously than pride! But every brief experience of being without it is a chance to feel an honesty, warmth and freedom which demonstrate that there is a different way to live, and that it can bring a sort of healing which pride cannot even imagine.

Humility is not necessarily the beneficial opposite of pride. Quite apart from the false humility which tries to camouflage pride and is often unconvincing, there is also a dubious form which if not itself actually sinful yet certainly opens the way for sins. This is a timidity which does not rebel against the wrong it suffers – and the wrong it sees done to others – or a compromise which will not stand up for its own values but conforms to wrongdoing and sin for the sake of belonging. True humility is a beautiful, strong quality, a realistic assessment of both one's own faults *and* one's real worth, which can be relied upon in trouble or success. It is essential to mature personal and spiritual life, a pleasure to see and to experience. And it is a gift which comes from the surrender of misplaced pride, and the acceptance of saving reality.

Avarice, or covetousness, and envy are the traditional 'deadly sins' which I believe arise out of loss. An avaricious person is greedy for possessions, a covetous one greedy for what others possess, an envious one actively begrudges the advantages or possessions of others. To these may be added jealousy, which is a passionate and disordered desire to keep what one has and prevent anyone else from enjoying it. Put together like that, do they not delineate privation and deprivation eating at the heart of security? If we were confident of being loved and valued, would we need to bolster ourselves so frantically with possessions, position and advantage? These attitudes reveal needs which are never satisfied, because the attempts at satisfaction are on the level of activities and possessions, but the needs are from the deeper level of being loved and being strong enough to love in response. The hole in the heart is never filled in this way, it just goes on hurting more and more.

Gluttony is the overindulged possession of food in particular – by its nature a transitory satisfaction! – and lust I have already described as a greed for substitutes, whether we only imagine them in compulsive daydreams or have the means to obtain them in actuality. The presence of any sinful attitudes related to getting and keeping points to the hidden possibility of our postponing the seeming satisfaction for a while so that we may catch a glimpse of the real need. I am not suggesting any cold-turkey method of doing without them entirely – that would probably only set off internal hurricanes and volcanoes which would be very difficult to handle, and would confuse the picture anyway. But we have to know what lies beneath our wrongdoing and sins if we are to lessen them effectively; or if we can find no cause for them in our wounds, we must know that they are truly willed, and therefore sinful in the starkest sense. If we look, just look without condemning or fighting, we will learn; and when we have learned, we will be better able to gain from both wounds and sins the knowledge, energy and individual qualities which they can release to us.

Once again, I am interested to note that the traditional 'mortal' or 'deadly' sins (which I have sometimes called sinful attitudes) stress the big, bad characteristics, the active wrongdoing. Pride, anger and the several forms of greed are all ways to put down, hit out or grab. Of all the list, only sloth is not active. But there are other attitudes which I think must be nearly as harmful, but which would more likely come into the 'weak and wobbly' category. Cowardice in the face of more forceful personalities or in situations where one feels inadequate, betrayal of one's own values under pressure from more general standards, a lack of trust when security and certainty are under threat – these seem to me to have, in the long run, the same separating effects as the more active sinful attitudes, and they are even more cramping. Perhaps they have not been examined in the same way because they are meaner and more humiliating;

perhaps when they have been looked at they have seemed easier to correct and not so 'sinful'. Well, I can testify that the struggle against them can be very long and hard; I think that they may possibly be less damaging to other people than, for example, pride and anger, but they are only a little less corrosive to the person who bears them.

But they too carry their hidden gifts. Every time we fall into cowardice we are shown how great is our need for trust, and each timorous impulse to withdraw from affirmation and action is an opportunity to acknowledge our fearfulness but to do what we know to be right anyway. Recent research into the factors that make up the 'altruistic personality', for example of men and women who risked their lives to shelter Jews from the Nazis, indicates that people often fail to respond to such challenges because they feel unable to influence the situation. Acknowledging such helplessness is the necessary first step towards developing an ability to participate, to co-operate with those who are stronger and more active, and to realize just how much strength and support can come from deeper within ourselves and through the help of the Spirit.

## Second harvest

It is in the richness, beauty and joy of the universe that we discover the breadth of life; but our own *depths*, and the depth of meaning and significance of our lives, are found especially in suffering, including that of sin. When we really do feel the misery of our hurt and hurtful interaction with others, when we feel the awful loneliness of separation from the God we yearn for, when we look at the inward gulf which divides us from our selves, we are drawn by the need to understand our situation and make something better of it. When we go beyond the preoccupations of our struggle with sin and guilt, and search more quietly for its root, it is our depths which we enter, and where we find a new sort of strength and patience. Then we bring this into our daily lives, to make a new breadth as well. There is a particular maturity which we can gain only through the humble recognition of our wrongdoing, the fear of actual sin, the acknowledgement of human vulnerability and the conviction of God's forgiving and sharing love.

I have never felt easy with the idea of bringing good out of evil – it seemed to me better not to have evil in the first place! More prosaically, that idea can be used to excuse wrongdoing and sin with an attitude of 'it doesn't matter very much anyway, because in the long run God will bring good out of it'. People are so expert at finding excuses. But the fact remains that we all of us do wrong; and we cannot just leave it at that, so must look for the good which there can be. My unease was lessened one day when I heard about an actor and his wife whose first child died and who named their second child Rowan – which in medieval usage meant 'second harvest' or, literally, 'aftermath'. I mused on that image and began to see, instead of a conjurer's trick of pulling a good white rabbit out of an evil black hat, a picture of the harvest of sin reaped, its seed spilling onto the ground to grow bitter tares again, but then a second harrowing, and sowing, and long tending, so that a second, fairer harvest could be gathered. If we do indeed bear our own harvest of wrong, not excusing it, or trying to escape it, or handing it on to others to suffer, but trying to live it with understanding and to change it, then we can bring good out of it at last. The final results of sin can be a chastened soul with more awareness of its need for God and more understanding of people who still struggle with sin, to a softer heart and an outgoingness towards others because our own defensive self-opinion has been eased. How much better – perhaps – if we had never sinned; but, in the aftermath, we can bring a deeper good, and maybe even a greater one, to life.

There are gifts to be found even in the dread into which our journey may lead us. We are beset by temptations to avoid our deepest dread. We cling to people and possessions and activity, and lose awareness of our spiritual possibilities; or we retreat into the infinite possibilities of our spirits and personalities and neglect the task of living them out in our daily affairs. 'Yet both of these are necessary to man in whom both must be fulfilled "according to the will of God". So it is by accepting our despair and entering into our dread, offering both to God as the truth about us, that His work of transforming them creatively begins within us.'⁶ In *The Concept of Dread* (*there* is an intellect pressed to observe the utmost paralysis of terror), Kierkegaard writes of the man whose journey, 'holding fast to God', takes him into dread again and again:

> Then at last the attacks of dread, though they are fearful, are not such that he flees from them. For him dread becomes a serviceable spirit which against its will leads him whither he would go . . . he says, as a patient says to the surgeon when a painful operation is about to begin, 'Now, I am ready'. Then dread enters into his soul and searches it thoroughly, constraining out of him all the finite and petty, and leading him hence whither he would go.⁷

I myself had a more Tolkien-ish image for this experience. All the fears, and self-justification and inner threats were 'hobgoblins' for me, vigorous, jabbering, dark feelings and thoughts which tried to scramble all over my mind. I used to sit on the side of my bed, gripping the edge of the mattress with both hands and staring straight ahead, both physically and figuratively. Hobgoblins always attack from the sides and behind, and they try to make you turn and fight them directly. Never do it! Keep turned away from them even if you cannot move, keep on looking ahead though there seems nothing to see, keep longing for the goodness and rightness which reaches out to you even when you cannot name it. The hobgoblins of temptation, fear and guilt cannot defeat you if you refuse to fight them; endure their screeching attacks while you yearn for goodness, and their strength will die. I am not sure when I began to give the name of 'God' to 'straight ahead', but I understood Frank Lake when I read this:

> To obey the living Truth when every fibre of one's nature protests is to enter a mental defile . . . The eye of the man of faith sees by night in his dreams, and by day in his projections, a variety of hostile creatures, but they fall away before him. His gaze is directed into the darkness beyond

them, where he has an appointment with Christ. He walks precisely by the light of faith . . .

There exists, then, a life of faith which stands upon the fact that God 'takes the things that are not' and fills their admitted emptiness with His fullness so that they walk through life paradoxically, aware, at one and the same moment and in every day, both of their natural condition of emptiness, hollowness, or apathy, and of God's gifts of fullness, solidarity, and passionate love . . . It is not within our prerogative to determine when this body of our humiliation, in weakness or aversion or perversion, shall be obliterated. Christian experience is well content with the paradox of divine strength made perfect *in* weakness.[8]

Oh, I can hardly claim that I am 'well content' with it! I wish I were different, I wish my life had been different, I wish I did not carry my weakness; but my wishes are mere wavelets flapping against me as I travel. I know that I am drawn by the greater strength of the Spirit, and usually I am able to trust it. I am like a rudderless, mast-broken craft being towed by a great ship with a clear, true direction. Perhaps it would be better to get there under our own steam, to feel mature, and competent, and decisive – perhaps. But it is the travelling and the destination which matter, not our own achievements as travellers. That has been worth learning.

## Celebrate the scars

The scars of old sin are not ugly, as long as it has been overcome or even if we are still trying to overcome it. The very humility that these scars cause, the willingness to believe that we could fall again, are valuable to us. Hidden sin is ugly, and unhealingly so as long as it remains hidden; but sin faced in contrition is potentially beautiful, because the soul as it will be when it is healed shines through the wound. Julian of Norwich said that the tokens of sin will be turned into honours in heaven; certainly they can be turned into a wiser and more generous humanity here on earth. 'In nature, in creation, imperfection is not a sign of the absence of God. It is a sign that the ongoing creation is no easy thing. We all bear scars from this rugged process. We can – we must – celebrate the scars. The alternative is to opt out of the ongoing work of Dabhar [the Word].'[9] That ongoing work can perhaps be evaded or ignored by people who are fairly comfortable with their lives. But the pain of wrongdoing and the sharper fear and shame of sin lead those who wrestle with them towards necessary change and development. In some, they serve as a hunger, which impels us to search for a wholesome food; in others, they are a torture:

> Sin is the sharpest scourge with which any chosen soul can be beaten, and this scourge belabours and breaks men and women, and they become so despicable in their own sight that it seems to them that they are fit for nothing but as it were to sink into hell; but when by the inspiration of the Holy Spirit contrition seizes them, then the Spirit turns bitterness into hope of God's mercy. And then the wounds begin to heal and the soul to revive . . . The Holy Spirit leads him to confession, willing to reveal his sins, nakedly and truthfully, with great sorrow and great shame that he has so befouled God's fair image . . . Every sinful soul must be healed by this medicine, especially of the sins which are mortal to him. Though he be healed, his wounds are not seen by God as wounds but as honours. And as sin is punished here with sorrow and penance, in contrary fashion it will be rewarded in heaven by the courteous love of our Lord Almighty, who does not wish anyone who comes there to lose his labours.[10]

Clearly, this can only happen when the sin is recognized and repented of, and the will united again with God. But the maturity which results from that truthfulness and effort can then receive and respond to God in a way which would not have been possible before the sin, its suffering, and all that followed.

### 'Yes' and 'No'

The attitudes which we need to foster, towards both other sinners and ourselves as sinners, are not exactly paradoxical, but they certainly feel like a contradiction, even an inner division, until we become skilled at them. The struggle with our own sin has two aspects, back to back like the two faces of one coin. The first part is the admission of the sin itself. People may often seem to be admitting what they do, but no relief or change of direction comes to them from it. Closer listening will reveal the qualifications which hedge the confession and blunt its transformative power. 'There's a part of me which always chooses to . . . ' 'I didn't consciously intend . . . ' 'I don't really mean to hurt you, it's just . . . ' 'I know that's what I did, but I don't really *feel* like that . . . ' There cannot be *any* qualifications. Despite all that I have said about the damage we may have undergone, our innocence and ignorance when we suffered it, and the way we had to protect ourselves, in the end – and in order to make a new beginning – we have to accept responsibility for what we, as adults, actually do with that damage. We have to start the change by acknowledging, as deeply and fully as possible, what we have done, and may still be doing. 'I did do it. *I* did it.' We have to start with that because there is no way we can take a second step without it.

But the next step is almost the opposite. 'I did that; yes, without any qualifying or blurring or excusing, I did it. But that's not all there is to me.' Our goodness is also present, and that, or at least our need for that, is what speaks. That is what has the strength to accept responsibility. That is what can forgive the harm done to us, and mend the harm which we have done. That is what welcomes God's unceasing forgiveness at last, and journeys towards him. These two movements, of letting in the truth and then moving beyond it to goodness, will have to be repeated again and again. Even when the first admission has been a huge uncovering, and the first affirmation a major change of direction, there will be a need to overcome perhaps years of habitual wrong attitudes and intentions. It is like learning and practising a new way to breathe.

We need a similar dual approach towards those who sin against us and ours. What they do to us or try to make us do may have to be utterly repudiated; we cannot take part in their wrong, either as accomplices or colluding victims (sometimes we cannot escape being involuntary victims). But deeper than the actions and even than the ego which chooses the actions is a spirit of goodness in them which we must always remember, look for and try to address. That is the seed from which change and reconciliation can grow.

All these efforts help to develop in us one of the most valuable gifts of the spirit, the quality of discernment. It enables us to distinguish between the person and the action, between actions arising from hurt and those intending harm, between failures, mistakes, wrongdoing, sin and evil. It gives us the confidence to judge the sin because we know we are willing to embrace the sinner, whether that is ourselves or somebody else. It is the quality which makes sense of, and makes possible, the powerful injunction 'Hate the sin, love the sinner'.

The wounds which drive people to sin, and the wounded life which their sin inflicts upon them, deserve our compassion, but hiding or protecting these wounds does sometimes lead to actual evil. M. Scott Peck notes in *The Road Less Travelled* that evil people 'hate the light and instinctively will do anything to avoid it, including attempting to extinguish it. They will destroy the light in their own children and in all other beings subject to their power. Evil people hate the light because it reveals themselves to themselves.' Ordinary wrongdoing, and perhaps even sin, is a passive failure to love; although it manifests 'nonlove', it is not evil. 'Truly evil people, on the other hand, actively rather than passively avoid extending themselves. They will take any action in their power . . . to preserve the integrity of their sick self.'[11] I would prefer to use 'sick ego' in this context; but I do agree with Peck. Usually the actions they take are well camouflaged, and sometimes evil actions are disturbingly interwoven with good ones in an individual, so that we have a great need for spiritual discernment in order to distinguish between sinfulness and evil – because compassion towards evil itself can never be appropriate.

## PARADOXICAL WOUNDS

There is nothing I can write here directly to any person who is doing evil things. Such people cannot be reached in their refusal and dishonesty; almost everything said to them or done to or for them is distorted and deflected, and is likely to result in greater harm. It is in their passing moments of unease or fearfulness that they may perhaps be touched by someone with perception and courage, but these will be opportunities which arise during the actual contacts of relationship, and I cannot attempt them in this book. I feel that whatever I say here can only be for those who live with or suffer from personal evil.

I have had to think very deeply about what can be done in such a situation. Priests and ministers, psychotherapists, professionals in the law, all have time-limited contact with evil individuals, and work within supportive and explanatory frameworks; the malign influence upon them can be contained. But husbands and wives, parents and children, have no such protection, and their need and effort to love the damaging individual is very strong. It may take many years of anguish to learn that direct human love is almost always twisted and exploited by the blackness in an evil sinner. I am afraid that in the long run the solution will usually turn out to be a radical detachment, or even separation. Evil exerts a moral – and emotional – contagion which must not be allowed to destroy surrounding lives.

But even in this case, the detached relative or lover must continue to love, because that is *his* or *her* goodness. We cannot love evil, we should not love the sin, it may even become impossible to love the sinner in his personality and intention. What is left? At last, only the paradox – the seeming outrage – of human beings loving without any human touch, response or relating, in a naked, suffering, horrified and compassionate love for the soul of goodness imprisoned and helpless within the evil loved one. We learn how to do without all the ordinary warmth of human love and to enter only into God's love and to rely only upon his hope. It is a harvest which the heart finds bitter indeed, but at least from the devastation there will have been *some* harvest.

## Embodying the vision

I believe that every one of us is an incarnation. We each have the opportunity to embody what is most Real and Right, and we have to resist embodying wrongness and untruth. What we make of our lives on earth can be our manifestation of God in us and of our relationship with him, or may express our refusal of both God and our selves, or is most probably a very human mixture of the two. In this effort, our understanding of what we are called to embody increases, and with it the realization of how far we and others are from fulfilling the vision. One of the characteristics of maturity is to recognize how great this disparity is, and yet to continue our work of incarnation without discouragement. Some people attain their perspective through the vision of Goodness and a slow conformity to it; others experience the darkness of sin first, and learn to see beyond that to the light of their goal. All will suffer the contradiction between the unacceptability of sin and compassion for the sinner, either by watching the door to evil opening in one whom they love and whose inherent goodness they know but can no longer reach, or by facing their own sin and its harmful and continuing consequences and yet still believing themselves forgiven and worth cherishing. Both the negative and the positive aspects are facts we cannot escape, and by our wrestling with them we turn contradiction into paradox. The boundaries of our personalities will be stretched until they break, to encompass it, but stretch they must.

In an article comparing Christianity and psychotherapy, Alan Wilkinson says that 'both are concerned to transform misery into pain. Misery is self-regarding, destructive and paralysing. Pain can be worked with at least in part and sometimes understood.'[12] And to the degree that it is understood and worked with, it brings us gifts of repentance, reparation, acceptance and growth. The paradoxical wounds drive us to find the true 'I' deeper than the wounded ego.

# 6

# A BLOW TO THE HEART

**Compunction**

There are times when the truth about ourselves suddenly breaks through our defences and evasions. It may be glancingly, in the middle of something else entirely, catching us from the side, under our shield; it may be an unexpected fall into a greater depth when we thought we knew, safely, how deep our tears and promises would take us. Like a blow to the heart, we are struck by compunction – not a mere regret, as about a white lie, nor an aching but passive remorse, but a sudden insight, stunning and undeniable, into the truth of our sin. In one movement, we are jolted awake to our present state, and swept by a vibrant yearning for the goodness we lack. Emotionally and spiritually, our breath is stopped by it; without enough warning, we find that a new start is upon us, and that we must make a choice.

Strange that it should be yet another wound which truly starts our journey; but compunction is indeed the wound of healing. 'Tears flow when the real source of our life is uncovered, when the mask of pretence is dropped, when our strategies of self-deception are abandoned . . . To come to this place where one is truly alive, one must hit rock bottom. There must be a breakthrough to the place of deepest helplessness.'[1] When some great trouble, conflict or distress breaks up our defences and pretences, we can no longer hide from our terror, pain and rage. When our own longing for forgiveness and reality presses upon us from within, we are offered a new life on a different foundation. For perhaps only a brief while, we have the chance to admit the truth about our inner being. We can confess to the shame about our weakness and to the lies which have propped us up; to our fury and jealousy and the way we have always blamed others; to all the tangles of our personalities and the wrongdoing and sin they have led to. The gift of compunction opens the path to new life.

But our own truth is always painful and difficult to affirm. We think that if only it were this or that other admission we had to make, it would not be so hard; we often try to get away with some admission less or other than the one asked of us. We fear that our strength will not be enough for whatever our truth takes us into, or we cannot see anything beyond it and dare not take such a risk. We do not recognize the gift, or realize what it brings to us. 'The soul is not a fixed entity . . . it is a movement that begins whenever man experiences the psychological pain of contradiction . . . But almost always, almost without any exceptions whatsoever, this new energy is immediately dispersed and comes to nothing. A hundred, a thousand times a day, perhaps, the "soul is aborted".'[2] How many times grace comes to us with opportunities for self-understanding, admission of the truth within it, and contrition for the wrong we have done or the good we have left undone. How many times the opportunities slip past us, in the routine of the day, the familiarity of ritual, the swift reaction of excuses, the habit of fearfulness.

Compunction opens our souls to us; when our hearts are pierced by the truth, God's love can enter them and make a deeper new life of the spirit possible.

> It is as if God has placed time-bombs inside us, programmed to go off at certain intervals in order to make a gaping hole in us so that we can continue to be open to life. He is always creating new space in us by means of these explosions. We are continually being given the space to choose either 'heaven' or 'hell', to act in such a way that we are either more and more curved in on ourselves or more and more turned towards God.[3]

If we do accept this explosive gift and all that it brings to us, we will then find the quieter spaces which God offers us 'a thousand times a day'. God's grace prompting to contrition and new life is always present, and willingly enters whenever a person is opened to it by thought and prayer, by the exchanges of human relationship, and all the events of daily life. We only need to welcome it and be willing to work with it.

Only! It will demand all that we are. Intellect, feeling, will and action are all called upon for a new life. Conversion and repentance are movements of the whole person. The intellect sees what harm is being done, the feeling spirit is appalled and repelled by it, the will turns away from it and chooses to do better. Repugnance without understanding cannot properly inform the will; intellect without feeling or the determination to change is merely analysis; an assertion of will without clear sight and directed emotional energy is likely to fall again into the habit of wrongdoing. Furthermore, the presence of the whole person presupposes an awareness of the whole situation – not, of course, in its hidden motivation and many details (that will have to develop over time), but a deep and quiet perspective upon the truth, or at least an ego-wrenching attempt to keep one's eyes open and to acknowledge the various dimensions of past wrongdoing. Erich Fromm stresses the importance of this quality, especially when we are dealing with the unconscious aspects of our contradictory inclinations: 'If we ask what factors support freedom of choice even if the irrational inclination is the stronger, we find that the decisive factor in choosing the better rather than the worse lies in *awareness*.' He says that we must be aware of what makes up good and evil, and of which action is most appropriate in each situation to achieve the desired goal. We need to be especially aware of the unconscious forces behind our evident desires, of the real possibilities distinct from the wishful ones, so that we perceive the real choices which are available, and to be aware of the likely consequences of each choice. And last of all, we need 'awareness of the fact that awareness as such is not effective unless it is accompanied by the *will* to act, by the readiness to suffer the pain of frustration that necessarily results from an action contrary to one's passions'.[4]

Compunction uncovers the painful sight of what we have become, in our wrongdoing and inauthenticity; but through it we also gain, or regain, the vision of what we *can* become – which deep inside ourselves we have always known, but have been unable to enjoy. 'God within us' is not an abstraction; it is the full and felt enjoyment of our own goodness working with his goodness. In the revelation which brought to Julian of Norwich her own compassionate understanding of sin, she saw a servant hastening to do his lord's will, and fallen into a ditch where he

> groans and moans and tosses about and writhes, but cannot rise or help himself in any way. And in all of this, the greatest hurt which I saw him in was lack of consolation, for he could not turn his face to look on his loving lord, who was very close to him, in whom is all consolation; but like a man who was for the time extremely feeble and foolish, he paid heed to his feelings and his continuing distress.[5]

He could see nothing but his misery, and guilt, and self-blame, and self-pity; he could not find his own good self. Grace Jantzen writes of Julian's realization that

> because of the blindness of our understanding, we are prevented from knowing the goodness of our own souls, and thus we despair. We feel guilty and alienated and utterly unworthy of love and unable to receive it . . . The blindness . . . is all too real; and it effectively prevents us from recognizing that at bottom we really do want to be good and to know the love of God.[6]

When we are lost in sin or crushed by guilt, we no longer believe in our own essential goodness or in the ever-present love of God.

When the sharpness of compunction restores our vision, we suffer the pain of seeing just how far our actions have fallen away from our goodness, but the goodness itself returns to our lives, and with it the possibility of new action which will affirm and express it. Remorse and regret are only a first, and passing, stage; the value of compunction is that it opens us again to our love for God, which we had forgotten or lost, and we can feel – perhaps for the first time – how *his* love surrounds us and can draw us out of our torture.

True repentance is no dreary, groaning state. It frees us from self-preoccupation, because what we have looked at with complete honesty and confession we need no longer examine. It gives us God's forgiving light with which to see our darkness, in place of our own harsh self-judgement; it gives us trust in God's goodness and in our own, responding to him. From it we gain understanding, sympathy and generosity, to enrich our relationships; and we lose the need to defend our wobbly self-images and touchy consciences. Hope, and vitality, and even some humour, are the fruits of repentance.

But we do need to be hollowed out before something new can grow. We have to put aside our defensive shields, and consciously allow a new kind of pain; we have to admit the truth about ourselves, and – *whatever* it is – that will hurt. Whether the truth is anger and hatred or weakness and cowardice, we will be equally reluctant to face it at last. And here we are, being asked not just to look at what we really have been and done, behind our disguises and pretences, but to admit to it, to own it as our action, our attitude. True and full confession is a scouring process.

None of us can escape it, for there is a sense in which we are all truly guilty. Those of us who have tangled our lives in defensive structures have been guilty of living lies; those who were crushed by inauthentic guilt have been guilty of not believing in their own goodness and innocence. Those who have raged and blamed were guilty of pride and retaliation; those who clung so needfully have also blackmailed; even those trapped in non-being have shrunk into their own nothingness, away from others and the pain which they cause. These have not been deliberate sins, often they were not even formal wrongdoing – but wrong has come from them. We have all wronged the image of God within us, in one way or another, and have failed in lovingness towards either ourselves or those who need love from us. But guilt, however authentic, is only the first half of the movement, for we are all truly good. That may be almost as hard to admit! We truly are the images of God; goodness, love and mercy are all within us, ready and able to grow.

## The pain of acceptance

Compunction scours away the sins of fear and anger which have eaten into us. We are left emptied, but frightened and uncertain in this unfamiliar sparse territory, anxious that the devils may return to the emptied space. And so they might, if we feared and watched them, but we are turned now in a new direction, and something else is offered to us. What we must allow into that space is acceptance – our acceptance of the truth we have admitted and of ourselves of whom it is true, and God's loving acceptance of it and of us. '"Behold I stand at the door and knock; if anyone hears my voice and opens the door, I will come in."[7] God knocks, but waits for man to open the door – He does not break it down. The grace of God invites all but compels none.'[8] We have felt compunction knock upon our heart, we heard God's plea, 'Repent, and let me in', and now the time comes for us to open the door to his acceptance. Morton Kelsey says, 'When real love does occur one finds that an individual is accepted by another person no matter what is revealed about that individual, and this kind of love is not easy . . . It is a very painful thing to be genuinely accepted. Then there is no reason not to look at oneself. All of one's excuses are swept away.'[9] Acceptance confirms the truth of what we have admitted, and removes the lingering option to run away from it yet again. It seals our fate. 'God offers us a more accepting love than any human relationship, and we actually shy away from it because of the deepening honesty and growth it requires, both of which involve shedding one's skin time after time.'[10]

So, with acceptance comes pain, yet again, but such a different pain. We feel ourselves stretching, where before we had been so stiff and resistant. We feel hope, that most aching and risky of all responses; we know we are no longer alone, but that means we must let the other into our hearts. We are beginning the pains of growth which opens us up. Now the time has come to allow God's acceptance, and to accept ourselves. We may even have to endure the terrifying acceptance of those we have hurt and loved; and a new cycle of being starts – truth and repentance, acceptance and more truth, repentance and love and more acceptance, and deeper truth with deeper repentance . . . Acceptance is a different sort of blow to the heart.

God knows all about pain; his love for us is rooted in the pain which our separation causes him. In its constancy which *will not* reject any part of the beloved, such a love loves all the reality of the sinner's life, can accept all its meanness and cowardice and pretence. Trusting to such a love, a sinner can dare to look at his actual life in all its detail and to accept that this is what is – because tangible reality is the only starting-off place for a new journey. But as soon as he or she does so, the details begin to change, and it becomes a different life. A life in grace, within grace. It becomes an awareness of the union which was always present to us but which we could not, would not, accept.

> God is gentle . . . He does not seem to worry about our past wrong-doing, even though its effects may still cause suffering to ourselves and others . . . What does concern him is the direction in which we are moving. If we turn towards him, no matter how far away we may be, he reaches out to welcome us. Our real sin is in refusing, or fearing to turn back, either because we are quite content with ourselves as we are, or because we think we must first put ourselves in order before we can turn to him.[11]

I doubt that anyone who was 'quite content' with him or herself would be reading this book; but many of us are likely to feel that we must be entirely changed and renewed before we can face God, or before he is likely to want us. We think of forgiveness as something we are given after we have changed. Well, that is true enough too often between people; but it is far from the truth of God's forgiving love. I hear Jesus saying 'You *are* forgiven'[12] – not will be, but are already, always have been. God has never been broken from you. Forgiveness here is not God's restoration to you of a place with him, because you are 'good' at last, but your own recognition that he has been with you through all the wrong which you have done. It was your sight of him that faltered, not his love of you. 'I saw truly that we are not dead in the sight of God, nor does he ever depart from us; but he will never have his full joy of us until we have our full joy in him, truly seeing his fair, blessed face. For we are ordained to this by nature, and brought to it by grace.'[13] You *are* forgiven: accept forgiven-ness. It is your inescapable condition.

We have been taught that when we repent, the spiritual slate is, so to speak, at last wiped clean; but I do not believe that is so. It seems to me that repentance is rather an experience of *realizing* that *the slate is clean*. 'In each soul that will be saved there is a good will which never assented to sin and never will.'[14] The incorruptible core of which Julian writes is God-and-us within us; and contrition opens that clean part to us, beyond all the blurring or fouling which we have done on and upon the other parts of ourselves. Our actions need correction, our personalities need maturity, our wills must be re-directed; but at our centre, born in us and never lost to us though so tragically often refused by us, is that core of goodness. Contrition is realizing the presence of our never-assenting good will *in sorrow for our betrayal of it*, and then we can bring our personalities and actions more into alignment with it.

**Visionary leap: cycles of improvement**

Something breaks through to us, in compunction; at first we only have to allow, and respond. But then it sets us the need to choose what we will do about it. The time comes when we must do our share, actively. A friend wrote to me about his efforts to give up blaming and punishing others without falling into discouragement and self-blame, and called this the time of 'acceptance without indulgence, and discipline without condemnation'. We learn to accept ourselves, without trying to evade responsibility for what we have done; we hold to the path and do what it asks of us, without the bitter scourge of the super-ego. However great the traumas were, however painful the scars or constricting the distortions, there is always some choice about not continuing to act upon them. It may be only in minor or peripheral aspects at first, but it will grow. Sometimes it cannot be more than a change of attitude, to start with, such as a decision not to lie to oneself about the sin even if one can only rarely resist doing it. Harold Kushner claims that 'to say "it is not his fault, he was not free to choose" is to rob a person of his humanity, to reduce him to the level of an animal who is similarly not free to choose between right and wrong.'[15] There is always some choice, though always at some cost.

Compunction liberates us from the grip of sin and its fears, and from real, but static, guilt. It liberates us for good and loving action. We can give meaning to whatever happened to us by asking, 'What am I going to do about it *now*?' When our hearts are broken open, this is the question which incarnation, the daily living of the Spirit, asks of us, and we create ourselves by our answers to it. 'We are hewn out of our possibilities by our choices.'[16]

The stage of compunction, of the blow to the heart, of heartbroken recognition of one's sin and its consequences, is followed by that of reparation and regeneration, when the repentant sinner starts a new growth of commitment and does whatever is possible to repair the harm caused by the sin and to embark upon a different way of life. But in actual experience, these are not so much two stages, one following the other, as two movements which may be expressed alternately and sometimes confusedly. The whole period of reformation is experienced as a mixture of the two movements which may seem at the time to have little pattern. But they can legitimately be considered as stages when they are viewed in the long-term, or when we look back upon the apparent confusion. At first, the movements of sharp repentance will be the strongest or most vivid experience, with groping, uncertain acts of reparation which seem to have little effect; but as we are confirmed in the new way, the pain of admitting to sin will ease, the confidence, willingness and effectiveness of reparative and regenerative actions will grow. The balance will swing from compunction to reparation, and to gratitude for the chance of reparation and new life.

Compunction probably will not be one overwhelming experience. Or perhaps it would be more accurate to say that even when the first experience *is* a tremendous reversal of our lives, yet we will probably have to reaffirm it many times before our new direction is assured; and for many people, a gradual way of change will be more natural and productive anyway. Any 'blow to the heart' happens suddenly, but its depth and transformative power will be different for various temperaments. There seem to be two basic ways for people to change, which I have called the 'slow and cyclic' and the 'sudden and straight'. I make no value judgement between them; they are just different ways for different people, or in different circumstances.

The sudden and straight way is truly an experience of conversion, of being turned right around. It is a sometimes explosive vision of a new life available, with a total commitment to it as the highest good, and may well precede any consistent personal ability to live it. It initiates a long period of continuing growth in which the vision most likely breaks through time and again with intensity and energy for change whenever the person has fallen away from it.

One might think that such a visionary way would be rather easy to follow, because of its intensity; but it has two serious difficulties. The blow of compunction causes a major dislocation in such a life, and demands a complete and ungrudging and immediate 'Yes', both inwardly and in action. It requires the sort of courage which leaps in response, and only discovers the cost afterwards. Then the next difficulty arises, for failure to live up to the vision – and such failures are inevitable – is very discouraging. The one who leaps forward is always at risk of being a backslider! Nevertheless, he or she is not one who is likely to change direction, because the vision never fades entirely. It continues to provide the motive and encouragement for the necessary psychological work of improvement and the willingly renewed action after each fall, until one *is* living it; and the commitment which came in the first intense experience provides a stability from which to make the effort. This way is what I would think of as *redemption*: that is, stepping into a new inner world and then, in hope and discipline, working towards the embodiment of the vision in one's own individual life. In traditional terms, it is a sudden reorientation of the will, to be followed by a long reordering of the affections.

A different temperament will not be so broken by compunction, and may have to respond more deliberately and determinedly. The confrontation with sin and weakness will come repeatedly, as it does to the visionary, but part of the work of change will be consciously allowing and helping each experience to be as deep and complete as possible, because the old ways will probably not have been fully exposed. They will keep trying to assert themselves and to block change, so they will frequently have to be re-examined. Instead of the leap and the risk of falling back, there will be more of a regular repetition. Time and again, sometimes hourly and daily, the individual has the opportunity to act differently in situations of characteristic wrongdoings or sin. But since it will only be a little differently, or only a moderate change, there is just as frequently the need to invite compunction actively, and consciously to make the comparison between the action and the very best one could have done. This way is basically cyclical, a matter of repeated confrontation with and steady improvement of characteristic weaknesses, failings and wrongdoing. It runs the risk of drifting off-course little by little, or of falling into compromise and accepting a lower standard than was offered in the first insight. I think that such a gradual development is epitomized by the doctrine of reincarnation, which describes the soul as slowly working through the consequences of actions performed in previous lives. Just as the other way could be seen as redemption, so this way is like *karma*, when through many lifetimes' improving quality of action, the eternal self is freed from the confining and distorting influence of its succession of false egos, and can realize its identity with divine reality. In this struggle, through many days and months of improving action the ego is freed at last from the confinement and distortion of sins, and the deeper self slowly comes into view.

As I have written elsewhere[17], these two ways of change are certainly not exclusive, though I think that an individual does tend to be a gradual or a sudden type. The latter will not have much control over the coming of the vision, but will then have to work deliberately at the gradual improvement of the laggard personality; the former generally works slowly and steadily at self-development, but will be required to respond to sudden opportunities for transforming choice. The gradual type must sometimes take a risk on an only partially-seen vision; the sudden type will need to admit his or her inadequacy for the vision and settle down to steady psychological work.

**The true self**

When our personalities are broken open like this, and we try to live from 'somewhere deeper', what we begin to find is the true self. There are a number of 'schools' which distinguish between the ego and the self, but I will not attempt an overview of transpersonal psychologies. Instead, I want to share the way *I* found that deeper centre in myself. It was truly a travelling, for I experienced the inner world geographically, with spaces, landscapes and objects, and I have drawn maps of wherever I had reached. The first one was very crude, just a central place, my ego, with a circuit of personality around it – no, let me go back even further, for there had been a time when there was nothing of me to be mapped or recorded in any way, no 'I' at all. I was at first just a defensive shell, my best hope to be at least an unbreakable one; and then that softened to a flexible, vulnerable membrane; but within, still – nothing. It was during a long psychoanalysis that I first felt that there was something precipitating out of non-being, a small, solid, something at my geographical centre, which grew and formed until I could feel my own physical shape containing it: I had become ego and body, and that first inner map could be drawn, just ego and personality. But before very long I began to feel most dreadfully cramped; this surely was not enough. My need for meaning and dedication was urgent and expanding. So my own time of vision and conversion had to break through, two years of turmoil and realization so flooded with light that I could see nothing clearly in it. But what I could make out became my second map, like a sixteenth-century approximation to the world, with the ego and personality delineated in some detail, as it were Europe and Britain with their cities, and far to the west a vague coastline drawn, the great *terra incognita* of a New World. I think it was Robert Sencourt who said that 'God has the strangeness of undiscovered islands', and that strangeness called to me.

I failed in what I tried to do then, failed during marital and mental breakdown, and a long period of nameless struggle. I was saved from foundering in the confusion by a friend's almost passing sentence, 'Such a clear case of something trying to give birth to herself', at the same time as I discovered the work of C. G. Jung. My friend had said 'herself', one word; but Jung wrote about the self as a new centre, about 'my self', two words:

> If we picture the conscious mind with the ego at its centre, as being opposed to the unconscious, and if we now add to our mental picture the process of assimilating the unconscious, we can think of this assimilation as a kind of approximation of conscious and unconscious, where the centre of the total personality no longer coincides with the ego, but with a point midway between the conscious and the unconscious. This would be the point of a new equilibrium, a new centering of the total personality, a virtual centre which, on account of its focal position between conscious and unconscious, ensures for the personality a new and more solid foundation.[18]

So the 'baby' was born, and I was able to mark a place in that unknown land, a vertical mark, a point of balance, a fulcrum named The Self. As I lived my inner experience – the wounds, the distortions – and tried to make personal and theological sense of it in the light of study and reason and in the surrender of prayer, my weight as a person gathered on that new centre. The small circle of the ego in the circle of the personality took its place in a big oval sweep of the individual psyche, and beyond that I came to sense a greater oval of my spirit which enclosed the whole and which was informed, through all its breadth, by the Spirit itself. At the farthest reaches of my map, or three-dimensionally in its greatest depths, my soul rested against God.

I clarified a great jagged area on the distant boundary of the psyche, a wasteland of silent infant screaming into which I sometimes fell terrifyingly and without warning, and I labelled it ominously, 'Here Be Mountains'. There was another, manageable, area between 'me' – that is, my ego and personality – and my self, a place where I settled for a few years between the hard travelling. I worked to make this part of my psyche usable, even productive, and called it, gratefully, The Homestead, the place of understanding. Its concepts served me well when I eventually tackled The Mountains.

The weight of both my practical and inner functioning swung, in time, over to the self. This is where my values were formed and my decisions made, in the new guiding and deciding centre for which my personality served as a competent and practical junior partner. During the following years the Mountains were scaled, their Chasm endured, until, like Columbus or Jacques Cartier claiming a landhold, my self looked out from them and sensed the unlimited distances of its new world, the greater oval waiting to be mapped, a whole unknown continent; and my self – not my ego – was its explorer. My self prayed, my self loved, my self suffered; and my ego still tried to make sense of it all, and got the daily living done, one way or another.

Can you see the map now? That first oval of the personal psyche, large though it seemed and years though it took to traverse, is enclosed within this measureless sweep of the human spirit co-inhering with the Spirit of God. The light of reason from the 'old world' cannot match the tide of light which flows from the Godhead in its distances; and God is its solid ground and its clear air. Somewhere in those long plains which I still have to travel is The Well-Spring, and some day [I will drink?] from it. I cannot yet mark its details on my map, [but 'Blessed?] Be Well-Springs'.

If you too choose to go into and beyond your w[orld?, you] too will find your own new continent. It will not be easy; in fact one thing I can promise is that the journey will be difficult, and painful, and demanding. But my other promise is that it will be rewarding in a way you cannot even imagine yet because it will be your own unique embodiment of the journey into God. Pledge yourself only to this first step of contrition and willing change, and the Spirit will slowly uncover your true self to you; and then you – as humbled and willing ego – will have the responsibility and the achievement of living out your self in the world.

It is not just a new place, or area, which opens out to us when we take this step, but also a new dimension. Height, breadth and depth define the *static material* of life; add time to the equation and life becomes *dynamic*. And then the Spirit gives life *significance*: it is the fifth dimension, where the self is particularly at home. Christopher Bryant called the self an inbuilt 'principle of order'.[19] It perceives that deep organic order in the universe which is the pattern of grace, the Great Dance. 'Grace danceth: I would pipe: dance ye all. Amen.' Then it is asked to respond. 'Now answer thou unto my dancing.'[20]

The commitment to a new integration changes our lives from ego-centredness to self-centredness (in an exact though less usual sense of that word). The salvation of the spirit, in the next stage, can then transform the whole of human existence to Reality-centredness. It is the self which longs for and responds to Reality, and once the individual has grown past ego-centredness and the self becomes his or her guiding centre, then the growth even from self-centredness is probable, as the self gives itself over more and more to God's Reality. Harry Williams is characteristically straightforward about this process:

> I shall find God within me all right. I shall find the love and joy and peace which is my truest self. But the discovery will for a long time be mixed with the discomforts of the

> journey. What in due time will happen is that slowly (though not gradually but by fits and starts) I shall become more aware of God's presence within and less aware of the turmoil of the journey because, having found my truest self as God's presence within me, I shall be able to accept and receive the more superficial aspects of myself with less difficulty and pain . . . They will begin to diminish and even disappear. In the end . . . I shall be so aware of God's presence within me that the rest of me will be totally transfigured by it.[21]

We may need to untangle our ego's reactions, or understand and give up its protections; but our greatest need is to gain, by these means, awareness of our true selves, and to develop that in faith. All the wounds and the defensive reactions to wounds which we looked at in chapter 3 were psychological. They happened to the personality, the emotional/intellectual/physical complex of which the ego is the executive centre. The damage there, or the rigid and locked superstructure of personality built upon the damage, or the complex of avoidances and satisfactions proliferating throughout the personality, can be so extensive and powerful that to the individual and his or her family and colleagues, even to a counsellor or psychotherapist, it may seem beyond remedy.

But I know that the personality and the ego are not the only aspect or level of the person. The hidden goodness and richness of every individual self cannot be destroyed except by that person's own rejection of them – though indeed, there are tragic cases when they seem as good as destroyed, for the individual is never able to pierce the layers of damage and uncover them. In most people, however, they can be reached; but the process will be costly, especially to the ego which must give up or lose all the defences and seeming advantages which it has locked to itself. For strength and encouragement in the task, Christians especially are promised that beyond 'this body of death' which our suffering or our sins manifest, there is a fullness of new life. But everybody who has some belief in the goodness of humankind, in grace and the loving mercy of God, however far out of reach that seems, can look beyond this first level of personality, and learn to see, recognize and assent to the movements of the true self.

The self is a paradox, experienced but never defined. Is it a part of us? Or is it God in us? I believe we cannot even phrase that as an either/or question: the self is both. When is a wave a wave, and when is it a particle? The answer depends upon where you are looking from and what you are looking for. So it is with the self. As part of our psychological and personal structure, the self is us, open to God. As part of God's relationship with his creation, the self is God-in-us, reaching into our lives. Both are the truth; both viewpoints work, both answer questions. Our problem is only how to carry both, in their paradoxical reality.

## Self and the two ethics

The self is not just something that happens. It has to be accepted and encouraged in order to be an effective influence upon our active lives. Tillich says that a person is 'able to determine himself through decisions made in the centre of his being'.[22] We do not create our 'selves' so much as discover, or uncover, them; but we create 'ourselves' as whole persons through allowing those central decisions to become conscious and by working with all our strength and intelligence to put them into action.

> The moral imperative is the demand to become actually what one is essentially and therefore potentially. It is the power of man's being, given to him by nature, which he shall actualize in time and space. His true being shall become his actual being – this is the moral imperative. And since his true being is the being of a person in a community of persons, the moral imperative has this content: to become a person.[23]

The goal is to be living from your real self, and living with others in relationship as real selves.

This goal of mutuality is capable of only limited realization, because there are many people who are unwilling or unable to share the intense Dance of Grace. But even alone one can start upon the dance, and now is your time to do that – though it will bring many difficulties and pains, which we will look at in the next chapter. It will probably mean going against or giving up many of the standards you have developed or tried to hold to, because they will have been formed in wounds, or to protect or avenge wounds – your own or others'. The 'old' ethic, of obedience, enjoined such qualities as selflessness, self-control, and self-abnegation; but these are, more accurately, efforts and characteristics of the ego rather than the true self. Too often, they are not signs of a glad and free service for a loving, accepting God, expressed in generous and flexible relationships, but are used as ways to maintain personal and social power structures. If the word 'ego' is substituted for 'self', the manipulation behind these injunctions becomes more evident. Ego-lessness in a young person, for example, is very welcome to a parent who fears the separation of growing independence – just as it is to an adult son or daughter whose dependence buys a mother's attention, and free accommodation in the parental home. Ego-control ensures that one's terror does not break through shamefully in public, or it pacifies a spouse who flares up at the slightest complaint. 'Self-abnegation' is a hard one to resist, for it is true that the ego must be denied and restricted, often; but the reason for this is so that the self may be affirmed and dedicated in action, not just so that the ego surrenders its autonomy, for example to a selfish and demanding elderly parent or a bullying colleague. We have to be very careful about these 'self-' words, and look at them clearly to see whether they are really being used as 'ego-' ones; but there will be a lot of pressure from many sides to retain the confusion so that these more superficial characteristics can seem to be the basis of a spiritual life, and obedience to the standards they portray can be required of us.

The ethic of creativity, however, does rightly make the true, non-ego self the centre, in self-awareness, self-understanding, self-acceptance and self-affirmation. Of these, only in self-acceptance might the word 'ego' more accurately be used, for it is the ego, with all its failings, which the true self accepts and works alongside. The self, being inclusive and welcoming, of course accepts itself! But more importantly, it accepts not only the one ego it lives with so intimately but also (though often with regret and much forgiveness) those many other egos with whom it has to deal. These qualities of the self all include ego in the sense that when we are truly aware of our selves we cannot be hiding or disguising our egos; when we understand the deep purposes and movements of our selves we see more clearly either our ego's conflict with these depths or its ability to collaborate with them; and when the self affirms us as whole persons it affirms the value of the ego which is such an important part of the whole. In these affirmations of the self there is no separating and excluding egotism, for the self truly is the personal aspect of 'that of God in everyone', and it is the self which makes the explorer's journey to God himself, recognizing and affirming other selves on the way. But the self's journey may involve heartbreaking conflict with those who require obedience to egotistical standards as the price for their Acceptance, Sustenance, and bestowal of Belonging, and both self and ego may sometimes find it a sad and costly journey.

But as we continue to examine our lives from the perspective of the true self, we become free to find our own understanding of what really is sinful, and to make a life according to our own values. Tillich says that 'being precedes value, but value fulfils being'.[24] In simpler words, what comes first of all is a person's essential being, who he or she is; but that being is not fulfilled until the person develops values and expresses them in living. A first requirement will be to ask whether or not we really are sinning! Is that what guilt is telling us? Is that what unhappiness or failure are telling us? If our self says 'Yes, it is', then we can draw upon the guidance and the resources of the self, in its life towards God, to help us do things differently. But the answer may be 'Yes, it has been', and will show the way in which the wrongdoing or sinful actions arose from the need for protection which is now less necessary or can be obtained in some less harmful way, or from a compulsive wish for revenge which is now amenable to choice and change. The answer, the requirements and the ability will all come from the self and its values.

If, sinning, we look towards the future, it is usually towards a false one, in which we will either retain the benefits of sin while being cleansed of its harm, or will become magically free of it; the view from within sin is always distorted and unrealistic. The view from the self is both more accepting and more demanding. The naming of our own values, and the attitudes and actions they imply, lays upon us a responsibility which we evade only with serious harm to ourselves. To our selves. This is the fifth dimension, and it has its own natural laws. Responsibility for the consequences of our actions is one of its greatest; and closely following upon that are the way in which responsibility increases with awareness, and harm to the sinner himself increases in knowledgeable sin. The view from the self opens a true future of real possibilities and real consequences, as well as real achievements. They must be taken seriously, but they can also be accepted gladly and with a willing response.

**Self-absolution and renewal**

A friend wrote to me during his struggle with sin, saying he knew that he was already forgiven by God, but that there was another 'absolution which comes after penance . . . it is self-absolution, which comes from knowing I have done what I can with the knowledge I've gained from the past'. Perhaps we could say that our self, mediating God's loving acceptance, absolves our ego; but whatever words we use (and I do not want to start playing with such words), the personal effect will be an inner ease and assurance. 'The terrible cycle of blaming others, of finding a scapegoat, of persecuting the marginal, is brought to a halt every time believers repent and accept their guilt.'[25] It is the *acceptance of guilt* (where that is deserved) which brings self-absolution. When we stop arguing with ourselves and other people about whether we really did it or not; when we stop being afraid of punishment and face the consequences instead; when we give the full name to our action, then we become willing to accept forgiveness, from God and from others, and we discover self-absolution. Another friend said that 'the radiation within us of self-absolution is unforgettable'. She believed that if a person really experiences that state just once, then its joy and relief bring the strength to search for and work for it again and again.

Self-acceptance and self-forgiveness are not easy; for guilt-absorbed or self-accusing people they are even part of the penance. Another part, and this is for all of us, is to make good as much as we can of the harm we have done. Our relationships, the way we conduct our lives, our goals – they will all change during this process. If we are fortunate, we are able to make good the harm where it was actually done, and those we love or are responsible for will benefit personally from the effort. Often, direct reparation will not be possible – and that in itself is a terrible penance; so then we must, instead, be glad to give our love and our care wherever else we can. How we live the future does change the past, at some level; and the future is what matters now.

Matthew Fox praises Irenaeus's theology because 'for him the fall is not a fall from perfection but a frustration of growth'.[26] The difference in emphasis is important. People usually look back to a golden time in the past, to a time before the Fall in Eden, to the Age of Gold in Greece . . . Clearly, human beings need to believe in a golden time, a perfect time; and it is natural enough for us to feel that this was in the past. Our own memories are of some personal time, perhaps as long ago as before birth, perhaps more consciously (though sometimes inaccurately!) in childhood, which was at least close to perfect. All through our adult life we are likely to have a feeling of going downhill. But it is not necessary to see the golden age as in the past. We can deliberately look in the other direction, and consider that this inner knowledge of a golden time may be our recognition that the *future* can be golden, that growing perfection is possible and that we can reach towards it. Then there is a turning of our sight from the past, from where we started and how we got here – from the wounds – to the future, to where we are going and how we can get there.

> The gulf between creature and Creator is not impassable, for because we are in God's image we can know God and have communion with Him. And if man makes proper use of this faculty for communion with God, then he will become 'like' God, he will acquire the divine likeness... To acquire the likeness is to be deified, it is to become a 'second god', a 'god by grace'. 'I said, *you are gods*, and all of you sons of the Most High.'[27]

We are born in the image of God; there is that of God in us, the part which Julian said never assents to sin. But to become 'gods by grace', to know that we are all children of the Most High, we must turn away from the past – from our immersion in the pain of our wounds, from our longing for a time before they happened, from guilt, and from sin and its hidden or open gains – and look towards a future where we will grow more like God because we allow more and more of him into our lives, and where we will not only overcome separation but will grow in likeness.

If you are no longer trying to deny past wounds, and to deny or escape present sin, but are looking at all of it with greater understanding, you can open to the future as a whole person, and your capacity for honesty and love will grow. Unacknowledged sin, fear and rage cause a 'contraction of the mind',[28] for we dare not look at it nor at anything close to it nor at life without it. Facing and letting go of sin results in an expansion of the mind, and indeed of the whole person. Your life now will become flexible – graceful in both senses of the word. Freedom from sin and guilt means the ability to love and to feel loved, to go out to God and to others and to come back to yourself enriched, in a new cycle of being and well-being.

If you do change your life and actions in the way I have described, it will be a change for the better. But it may not seem to be so, according to your present standards. I can promise that 'all shall be well' – but quite possibly not as you at present define 'well'. Julian probably was not referring to familiar definitions either, though she did not spell out the differences as I am trying to do. Repentance will not take away the sin and leave you as before except that you will be minus the defect. It will change the structure of your personality, the balance of forces and shapes within you, so that you will have to learn all about those changes and grow into them – only to find then a changed set of weaknesses and temptations, and a new struggle! It does not really stop, you see; growing does not stop. The difference after repentance and reformation is that the struggles become more challenge than obstacle, and the sense just of growing becomes more sustaining and heartening. The struggle with sin becomes a growth beyond sin, but I cannot honestly assure you that the effort therefore becomes less; it just becomes different, and more worthwhile.

# 7

# LETTING GO AND LOSING

**From a negative way to a Via Negativa**

Sin is a negative way of living. If we do not consciously suffer from it ourselves, others certainly do, and its hidden effects undermine the integrity of our characters so that we dare not look at ourselves and will not let others see us. What we seem to gain from it actually diminishes us, and our energy, love, and creative possibility are sapped by it. If we are early-wounded, this negativity will have been involuntary at first; but we have seen that it does bring an appearance of safety or revenge, which is often retained even when some choice becomes possible and the sinfulness in it becomes more open. But when compunction has at last shown us to ourselves, if we continued to repeat those choices with open eyes we would be in far greater danger of psychological and spiritual harm.

> As long as we are ignorant, nothing is asked of us, but as soon as we know anything, we are answerable for the use we make of that knowledge. It may be a gift, but we are responsible for any particle of truth we have acquired: as it becomes our own, we cannot leave it dormant but have to take it into account in our behaviour, and in this sense we are to answer for any truth we have understood.[1]

So the time has come for the risks of growth. Letting go of sin, and working through the barriers of guilt, enables us to move on into creative and generous love and life, bringing richness to ourselves as individuals and to everything around us. Most of us realize that; then why is it so hard to choose? Because growth is risk, and effort, and sacrifice – which sin has enabled us to avoid.

It is exactly that unknown, that growingness, that uncertainty about what we will have to do and whether we will do it well and what demand will come next, which we fear. But 'faith is the readiness to go forward without certainty'.[2] Sin is, after all, a fairly predictable state, however miserable it occasionally becomes; and growing out of sin is at the very least unpredictable. It can be downright terrifying! It is also hard and slow, for most people. The struggle to resist and admit to sin and to guilt has been only a first step; and probably even so it will have to be repeated over and over again, because growth rarely happens in a neat series of completed stages. But whenever it happens and however long each happening is, this first period is a time of clearing the ground as we travel, and it cannot be shirked or skimped. 'One of the tasks of the way of illumination', says Christopher Bryant, 'is to deal at a deeper and more effective level with the obstacles to the journey with which the pilgrim had contended earlier on.' He warns against the distrust which makes us unwilling to commit ourselves further than we can see or predict, but 'progress in the pilgrimage demands *growth towards unlimited commitment* . . . As a person advances in the way of illumination, he comes to see with increasing clarity and conviction that the way of death, of letting go of self-interest, of concern for success or reputation or popularity, is the way to more abundant life.'[3]

The merely negative way we have been living has to become a true Via Negativa, in which we let go of our false securities and satisfactions, our ego-supporting view of ourselves, our rooted pride and selfishness, so that we may travel. We must actively co-operate in what will seem like our death. 'Except a corn of wheat fall into the ground and die . . . '[4] But it does not die. The *life* which is in the corn not only continues in the ground, but expands; it is the *form*, of the corn and of the life, which changes. The protective husk rots, the nutrient bulk is consumed, and the embryonic germ grows. There seems to be death; and we will seem to die. How much the change in the corn which we are is felt as rotting into nothing, as being consumed to nothing, or as growing into something new, will depend upon how much we are identified with each part. If we are very conscious and can identify with the whole corn and all that happens to it, then our experience will be of two concurrent processes – disintegration, as the husk of our protective structures falls apart and our egos are consumed, and a more enduring sense of integration as the embryonic self grows through its changing life. But most of us most of the time will experience one aspect more than another, and one after another, and will have to make what sense we can of the contradictions, and endure the tensions. Bryant offers guidance when reliance upon God rather than upon pride or self-control brings a greater awareness of repressed fears and hates now surging into consciousness:

> Alarmed at these threats to his integrity he will be driven to trust God as never before. As he learns to rely on God increasingly he becomes aware of the principle of order at work within him spreading the sense of security. Gradually, with many alternations of calm and storm, assurance grows in him. Growth in freedom like growth in faith cannot be painless; it is 'the time of tension between dying and birth'. It is the steel of the wounded surgeon which with sharp compassion he plies to cut away the adhesions which hinder freedom.[5]

We are to say, as Kierkegaard said, 'Now, I am ready'. It is good for us to welcome the steel as much as we can, to let go of our resistance and to do the new thing, whatever it may be in each situation. It is good for us to open just a little more than we had thought possible, so that more of the knots and tangles may be uncovered and cut away. The more we who are wounded actively co-operate with our selves as they unbandage yet another bruise or ulcer on the ego, and with God the compassionate surgeon, the more we can become aware that we are responsible, choice-making collaborators with him, and will find a new, reliable source of self-respect and acceptance.

Of course it will hurt; I do know that. 'Sacrifice is the act by which evil is changed into good; he who, under God, performs the act is sacrificed.'[6] Letting go is sacrifice, it is the repeated act of giving up whatever we had gained – power, safety, satisfaction, comfort – and as we do that we give up bits of our egos. Until we know the difference, it will feel like giving up bits of ourselves; and *we* are the ones who must do it. The time may come later – and it may come upon occasion even now – when God will do it for us, when we look and realize with relief and gladness that the running sore has been healed in the darkness; but first we must learn and demonstrate our willed and active co-operation with the Spirit.

And now is the time. Now has to be the time, because we never know how much time is left. Dag Hammarskjöld says that 'there is a point where everything becomes simple and there is no longer any question of choice, because all you have staked will be lost if you look back'.[7] However much you may want to believe that it is not now, that you will understand more clearly next week, that you will be stronger for the sacrifice next month, however much you want to pretend that the situation is complicated and still needs to be considered, it has to be now, because one simply cannot know which hour is the point of no return. When the sin, or sins, have been seen and named, and the decision made to move away from them, then the commitment is to the move itself, and there can be no willing return to the sin without betrayal. Once our hearts are opened and we are able to see, the imperative is growth, because the alternative would be decay.

## New yeast

There are new, or changed, qualities to help in growth. The most necessary and valuable is honesty. Whether we have closed our eyes in fear or fury, whether too proud to admit shame or too threatened to face non-being, we have lied; and 'the truth shall set you free'.[8] The first honesty is confession – which is nothing more than admitting what we have done, without justifications, excuses or omissions – whether to a priest, a therapist, a spiritual companion, the person who has been wronged, or simply to oneself: whoever the human listener may be, it is also God we speak to. In the first brokenness of compunction we may have named our sin with great accuracy. But however much relief repentance brought, or however glad we were to glimpse our hidden goodness, the sustained sight of this truth about ourselves is hard to take, and the temptation to blur the picture may grow very strong. But words matter, because they reflect realities, and the words of confession must be used with unflinching honesty. Not 'I didn't really say what I meant', but 'I lied'; not 'I was anxious and couldn't do it fully', but 'I funked it'; not just 'I want (or even need) this love affair' but also 'and I am risking my marriage with it'. Nobody loses more from such pathetic lies than the liar himself, for self and God are lost in them, and only the ego is fooled. There is a quality in ourselves which finds it harder to go ahead with wrongdoing and sins which have been clearly named, and we should make use of its help. John Sanford claims that psychological honesty and self-knowledge are the keys to a moral life founded upon inner truth:

> Most of us hide our duplicity from ourselves by using euphemisms instead of the real words for things we cannot face up to . . . psychological honesty is of fundamental importance to spiritual and psychological development. Without it nothing can take place; with it there is always the possibility that God . . . can break through our egocentricity and make something of us.[9]

Sanford is either too gentle in his reference to things we cannot face up to, or is himself not using words with full accuracy. We use euphemisms also for the things which we can, but will not, face up to, and 'cannot' is one of the most common of them.

Honest confession is a lifelong process; none of us can say it all once and for ever. And sometimes we really cannot; but it is a dreadful shame if we lose any part of the freedom which can be ours because we *will not* endure the pain of honesty.

Hope and trust are potent yeast . . . But how can I exhort you to turn to the qualities which I so miserably fail to develop myself? And yet perhaps for that very reason I know their value. I know also that we cannot command hope as a feeling, as a gladness or a willingness, but I have learned that we are almost always sufficiently free to remember it as a fact. In my own despair I found the philosopher Gabriel Marcel: 'Hope quite simply does not take any heed of the sum total calculation of possibilities on the basis of accepted experience.' Nor is it personal, as in 'the inventor or discoverer who says, "There must be a way" and who adds: "*I* am going to find it". He who hopes says simply: "It will be found".'[10]

It will be found, it will be done. We are not the only people, the only agents, the only energies, in the universe; in sheer reason we cannot deny that another person, or an unknown situation, or the energy of the Spirit, may act, and change this state in which we despair. For me, even at the very worst, hope is the admission that others exist and may act; it is especially the humble, reasonable admission that I cannot know what action the grace of God will take, and then the willingness to wait – even if I can face only a very little while longer – and to look for signs of that action, within me or outside. 'At the root of hope there is something which is literally offered to us: but we can refuse hope just as we can refuse love.'[11] Our problem is too often that we hope for some specific wanted thing, which we may very well know in our hearts is not possible or right, so that it is already a false hope. But if our hope is only *that God will act*, it is as much a certainty as a hope, and the only question left is whether we will refuse or accept what his action brings to us. 'Forget the former things,' he tells us, 'do not dwell on the past. See, I am doing a new thing! Now it springs up; do you not perceive it?'[12] Be ready for the new thing.

I am not sure how justified Matthew Fox is when he re-translates Jesus' words, but I like what he says anyway:

> The trust which is demanded in the darkness of the Via Negativa also heals. 'Go your way. Your trust has saved you.'[13] Trust makes whole. Not only the trust of ecstasy and delight as in the Via Positiva, but trust of the darkness,

the sinking and the nothingness of the Via Negativa . . . Trust drives out fear, and when we let go of fear we are ready to live fully, love fully, and be instruments of healing or salvation.[14]

## The discipline of letting go

This is a difficult part of the book to write as though I were the knowledgeable author. I find that I am less and less describing a mapped geography and experienced path, and am more aware of being on the road with you, limited to the perspective of the immediate difficulties and challenges. Whatever one's road has been – sin, or service, marriage, solitude, privation, creation or endurance – every road requires the discipline of letting go. 'We can set no limits to the tearing up of roots that is involved on our journey into God.'[15] Even today, as I write, I must name to myself the things which I have to let go of if I am to continue travelling; and of course I am reluctant. Of course you are too. But God surely knows how the human heart can ache and hang back. Perhaps he has a special joy in those who leap towards him reckless of cost or effort, but there must also be a tender and understanding welcome for those who have dragged themselves out of their reluctance and fear because they yearn for him so needfully. To let one's ego be consumed, be the sacrifice, 'is not an appeasement of the gods or of God, but a burning out of our own reluctance to let go.'[16] We have all too easily, throughout the history of humankind, projected sacrifice onto something outside, onto an animal to be slain in front of the altar, a Christ to die for our sins. But someone or something else, whether material or spiritual, can only be the symbol of what must happen inside us. It is our own egos, with all their fears and hopes, which we must sacrifice, in order to reach the reality of our true selves, and to live that with God.

For 'ordinary' people with ordinary bad habits or moderate failings, it may be enough to give up specific actions and to improve this or that attitude; and they may even, by this quiet route, discover that they have become their real selves. For those of us who have lived very wrongly, been very wounded, or need God very deeply, modification cannot be enough. We need transformation. It is not enough to let go of our sins; we must deliberately give up our damaged, distorted egos – which seem to be ourselves – in order to uncover our true selves at all, and to see our sins with any clarity. How deficient the English language sometimes is! We say 'I must lose myself' and it sounds total and horrifying; if we could say 'I must lose my-I in order to gain my-self', how much more accurate the statement would be, and more possible and desirable the action would be. But even giving up my-I turns out (though sometimes in the rather long run!) not to be total; it just feels that way at the time. Every time. 'He who is willing to lose his life shall find it: the losing is transitory; it is the finding that is permanent, eternal.'[17] Here I *am* speaking from a long experience of the road and can say with certainty: the ego is not actually lost, it is re-found at the end of the process – each time – cleansed and functioning anew with a different strength and a greater realism; but it must really be given up. You can cast your bread upon the waters with the hope, the trust, even the conviction, that it will be returned to you; but you must *cast* it, out of your hand and onto the chancy sea.

This is true of giving up both damage and sin, but there are different sorts of resistance in sin. In some people, the many tentacles of their sinfulness can have a most tenacious, sabotaging hold upon their personalities. Everything they do is blighted by it. They are not capable of fighting against such a pervasion of the ego; the only health they can achieve is from a repudiation of the battleground entirely. Although for many, and perhaps most, people it is enough that the ego should give up its wrong desires and harmful goals, in some the ego is crippled, taken over by pride and fury, or pulverized by the terror of desertion. It does not serve as a practical executive centre to manage a good-enough human life, but exhausts all the person's energy in struggle, damage, useless remorse and the magnetic pull of repeating the cycle. In such a case, the ego itself must be given up or the soul will be poisoned almost to its death.

The real self moves to the fullness of God's current. It can be tightly hidden but is not damaged by the traumas of infancy, nor possessed by unreal compensations. The real self must become the centre of life, the deeper fulcrum of balance and place of choice, and that cannot happen while a sickened ego fights with it for supremacy. Beyond even 'Not my will, Lord, but thine', the individual with an ego crippled past healing itself must beg 'Not me, Lord, but you'. The 'me' has to be handed over entirely, so that the self, and the love of God in which it has its being, can take up the direction of that person's life.

What appalling suggestion am I actually making? 'My ego is *me*', I seem to hear you object in outrage. 'It always has been. I can't live without it!' But Jesus has already said so: 'Unless a man give up his life . . . ' We have to realize that he meant exactly what he said. If an ego is so damaged or depraved that it prevents the livingness of God in the soul and the expression of God's love in action, it must be given up, however much that feels like tearing oneself into pieces. That is, so to speak, an inaccurate feeling; it is an egocentric one. Because I can promise you this: as the inner self unfolds within the seeming wreckage, it brings a perspective and abilities unguessed at by the clamouring ego, and from it as it grows into one's daily life there flows a slow healing of the ego, at last. But only after the ego is lost can it finally be found, in its true place and proportion and freed of its distortions and swollen demands.

One cannot, of course, let go of one's ego as though it were a cabbage one could pick up from the worktop and drop into the bin. One cannot say, 'Today I will give up my ego' and whoosh, it's done! Contrasting the ego and the self makes a vivid image, but it might be more helpful to speak of giving up egocentricity. With every opportunity to choose between asserting or letting go of ego-centred defences and satisfactions, we have chances to recognize how enclosed and blinkered we are, cut off from other people in heedlessness or false attentiveness, from our deeper selves in narrow interests and limited goals, and from God in fearful ego-regarding unwillingness. That in turn opens us to the chances to choose a wider and more significant action on each occasion. John Sanford calls it 'a willingness to give up egocentricity in order to serve God'.[18]

Beyond the specific wrongdoing and the sinful actions, there must be a letting go of sinful attitudes, and this will prove to be an even longer discipline. Clearly sin itself is egocentricity, but so is preoccupation with sin. It would be no use giving up a wrong action if one never stopped thinking about it afterwards. This is true not only of temptation, but less obviously of remorse for sinning, over-concentration on its effects, or fear of its recurrence; repentance can be prolonged, can become ego-regarding, can even become ego-inflating – and can be used to escape reparative action. We must let go, also, of the need to apportion blame, our own or others', before we are willing to act. We must even let go of our guilt, for guilt can be nursed at the expense of good action. We must recognize the temptation to let go of something less than the real sacrifice, trying to fool our selves and God with a substitute. If we are to be free of the sins which arise from defending our vulnerability, we will have to let go of being safely alone. It would also be wise to let go of any picture we have of ourselves as very improved, as perhaps past the danger of falling. 'If there be anywhere on earth a lover of God who is always kept safe from falling, I know nothing of it – for it was not shown to me. But this was shown: that in falling and rising again we are always held close in one love.'[19] We can always rise again; but we should know that it is God's love and our responsive selves which make that move, and not our incapable egos.

Strangely, it may be difficult to let go of weakness. The reason, as so often with other attitudes, that we hold on to our weakness is that it exempts us from action – right, reparative, strong action. Matthew Fox tells us that the Via Negativa carves a salvific gift of strength in us. 'Strength is, after all, a letting go of weakness, of self-pity, of puerile shame, of fear to be different or to be ourselves. Such strength saves. Not only oneself but others.'[20]

On the other hand, we must be alert to a particular false strength. Do you notice the great difference between 'letting go' and 'resisting' or 'fighting against'? Remember the hobgoblins? If you turn and fight them directly, they are bound to win. Fighting against sin is still being preoccupied with sin – and sometimes all that the sinful system needs is a preoccupation which ensures its own continuing existence. And while you resist, you can believe that you are demonstrating your strength; but it is a false impression, for the sin which so engages you is feeding off your attention to it. But exactly because the battle is a defence against the underlying pain and fear, it may be easier than letting go. The enemy is no longer gripped in your assertive hands, they are empty and uncertain. They must do something else, and that is an insecure feeling. It is frightening to let go of the past and let the present happen and let it grow into a future.

## Sacrificing our satisfactions

Much sin is not just a primary defence. It also brings satisfactions, if only the satisfaction of being successfully defended. Feeling stronger or cleverer than others, being too unwell to face demands, gaining approval, being the centre of attention, getting the last (and most stinging) word, escaping responsibility – the list is almost endless, and I have not even mentioned any of the more obvious advantages, like sexual pleasure in promiscuity or affluence in fraud.

One particular dear friend of mine has demonstrated, over a long time of great but misdirected effort, one of the most important aspects of wrestling against sin: you have to want to be free of it! That means you have to be willing to give up what you get from it, even unconsciously. (And one of the major difficulties of the struggle is that what people get out of sin often is unconscious.) After he eventually became aware that the hidden gains in an apparently miserable and defeating situation were contemptuous superiority, power to hurt others, and escape from mature commitment, the next stage of his struggle was to admit how much they mattered to him. This became the time of a change from excusable wrongdoing to a much deeper responsibility for culpable sin. When you realize that what you are doing is very wrong – and in this case other people were often being badly hurt – then you, quite simply, have to stop. If it seems that you really cannot stop, the first question to ask is: what are you getting out of it?

People get, and apparently value, some pretty odd 'secondary gains' from sin. My friend wanted to be miserable and incompetent; that effectively hid, even from himself, the deeper satisfaction he gained from being able to deprive others of the well-being which his success would bring to both them and himself. What he had to let go of was both an exploitable self-image of well-intentioned inability, and an actual situation of well-camouflaged destructiveness; and that is proving to be a very long struggle indeed.

What we often gain is escape from fear. We would rather be bad than weak and rather fight guilt than suffer fear, because our great guilt demonstrates how big and strong our sin is, and by association so are we. But our fear would reveal our weakness and vulnerability, and to a wounded ego that seems the worst situation of all. Interestingly, my friend did prefer to claim the weakness of incompetence and failure rather than admit to the strength and power of his destructiveness, but even that was only a seeming weakness, a clever use of camouflage to escape responsibility. I have little doubt that if he does sacrifice that too-satisfying power, he will begin to discover a more real and frightening vulnerability. He said that the greatest pain he has ever known has been allowing God's love to touch him. Allowing any touch upon our vulnerability is terrifying, even love's, even God's. We would rather maintain any lesser, and therefore more controllable, situation.

Why should people ever be willing to give up such useful, and often even enjoyable, gains? My friend's reason was typical. Beneath his camouflage of mere misery, and beneath the destructiveness which that hid, he was truly desperate and unhappy. He knew in his heart that his guilt was real, however much he lied about it; and he felt most painfully his isolation from God. Ultimately, sin is not satisfying. However strong the grip of the secondary gains may be, the lack of inner satisfaction and integrity is painful; and the gains become less satisfying as awareness grows of another, more worthwhile dimension which is being harmed by the sin.

## Realignment and persistence

Letting go is not passive. We have to open our hands, and put out of them what we have held onto. Letting go is a self-discipline initiated by the individual in response to the compunction which turned his or her life around, a positive and persistent effort to strip away emotional and material hindrances to the journey.

> This stage in our spiritual journey may last weeks, months, years or even a whole lifetime, depending on how seriously we take the consequences of our conversion and just how deeply the major sins are rooted in the soul. God's grace is present for us to make progress, but it requires our active co-operation and willingness to enter into the experience of 'night', albeit of a preliminary intensity, before any movement forward occurs.[21]

This *is* a night. Often we cannot see any goal, nor even understand what is happening. Sometimes we cannot see or sense God, and we lose awareness of our selves. We have nothing to depend upon except teaching which no longer has any savour, although we may not (at least yet) have to deny it, or upon the encouragement of friends who, for the present, see our road more clearly than we do. There are times when we have nothing at all to turn to but the memory of the vision, and a fidelity to it even when it seems utterly lost to us. 'If it was true when I first saw it, then it is still true, even though I can't see it now', is the best we can manage. So we hold to that course, either doggedly or desperately, until in some blessed hour we can see again and take fresh bearings.

John of the Cross devotes most of *The Ascent of Mount Carmel* to the description of this period of active discipline. He was writing for professed religious, and particularly those who are called to mystic contemplation, rather than for struggling sinners in the modern world; but I see a strong parallel. I have been describing an active, willed, sinner-initiated surrender of both the evident and the hidden gains of sins, and of the safety of pride and other defensive states of sin, and I have been encouraging you to enter upon the darkness and risk of a road you can barely see. 'The active night of the senses which follows conversion is a period of reform in which the priorities of the sensual soul are assessed, found wanting, and changed.'[22] In this academic definition by Desmond Tillyer we can recognize the process we have been looking at in this chapter. Certainly there has been an assessment of psychological priorities – 'psyche' means 'soul', and especially its emotion, memory, understanding, desires, etc. There has been understanding of the ways in which earlier and now exposed priorities fall short of the love and creativity we are capable of, and examination of the ways in which we can change. Letting go is a time of 'stripping away . . . of sensual hindrances to devotion'[23] – and truly we have been looking at some major hindrances. But John of the Cross realized that in this stage his readers still rightly appreciated and used the 'senses', which are not just the five physical senses but all feelings, abilities and qualities related to them, and I also want to affirm their beauty and value in all parts of our lives. St John allows that these 'faculties' of the soul may be used by the religious, though only if directed towards God; in the struggle against sin, our requirement is even more basic – we must not misuse them. We certainly need not try to cut them off or crush them down, but we should not misuse them to egocentric ends. Our task now is to bring them into alignment with the 'path of righteousness' which we have set upon, into alignment with God's will uncovered to us by grace.

This active co-operation with grace is the beginning of 'the purgative way, in which the pilgrim is especially concerned with facing and learning to overcome the inner hindrances to the heart's pilgrimage'.[24] It may be long and hard, but it is also marked by effective changes in ability and by visible achievements.

In the final analysis, the effort not to sin is an act of courage. It is taking a risk on God and being willing to do without one's props and secondary gains, it is looking at what one has become as a result of sin (that in itself needs intense courage) and trying to become something unknown. Courage like this is *self*-affirmation, instead of ego-assertion. 'The courage to be is the ethical act in which man affirms his own being in spite of those elements of his existence which conflict with his essential self-affirmation.'[25]

## The darkness of losing

For most of us there will be times during this stage when all our active ability fails us. It is not that we lose the willingness to change, but that our energy for it seems to miss its direction or to die away; even when we are not drawn back to the wrongdoing or sins, we find no momentum in ourselves for the way forward, and are afraid that we will relapse into the old ways. The new ways we have developed to deal with ourselves (with 'our-egos') and with other people seem to become less effective; prayer is more difficult and less often brings insight or courage; we are confused and anxious about our goals. Our hard-learned new discipline seems to fail us, and that is very frightening.

A person may have worked hard to gain considerable understanding of himself and of what he has done and why. Thinking and understanding are the strengths which, lacking a reliably useful impetus from emotion, he depends upon. If a time comes when he cannot get anywhere and cannot see why not, when it is not possible to understand what is happening in him, he will be disorientated and discouraged. Desmond Tillyer says, 'The mind cannot think, nothing "adds up", all satisfaction is destroyed, all sense of direction is lost, God seems unreal, all intellectual constructs supporting faith come crashing to the ground.'[26] A different sort of person will have had much help from the release of positive emotions and their energy, and have been able to combine this with thoughtful analysis well enough to form a new integrated picture of herself. When emotional enjoyment fails her, she may be able to ease the loss with continuing observation of her condition; but she will nevertheless feel flat and let down, and equally discouraged.

In either case, we blame ourselves for what seems like failure, after our turning away from the old ways and our attempts to live differently. It is easy to believe that we are losing the fruits of our effort, or are mistaken in what we are attempting. Therefore it is very important to know that times like this are both natural and deeply valuable. There is only so much we can do for and with ourselves, however willing we are, only so much which we have the power to let go of actively. There are other depths and darknesses which we cannot lose unless God works silently and painfully within us, cleansing us of weaknesses and wrongs which we cannot even know are there. It is a help to realize that there are legitimate times when the effort to free ourselves is no further use, but that we are then called to a simple and quiet trust. We must wait upon the Spirit in patience and hope, knowing that the Spirit always acts, and that our conscious awareness and understanding of that action are sometimes quite irrelevant. At these times, God's grace is reaching into us, flowing through us, in a new, different way, for new and unexpected ends.

> As the flowing of the ocean doth fill every creek and branch thereof, and then retires again towards its own being and fulness, and leaves a savour behind it; so doth the life and virtue of God flow into every one of our hearts, whom he hath made partakers of his divine nature . . . Stand still, and cease from thine own working, and in due time thou shalt enter into the rest, and thy eyes shall behold his salvation, whose testimonies are sure, and righteous altogether.[27]

The tide may come occasionally or frequently over a period, and such periods may recur; in a few people they will develop into a new spiritual state which will be very important for that person and will need to be understood as a stage in a mystic journey, which cannot be the subject of this book. But in everyone, the growth in discipline and the hidden losses at God's hands will together result in at least a change of timbre. Christopher Bryant describes the difference:

> The journey is from the outset a journey of faith; but in its earlier stages the traveller tends to be occupied with the hindrances to the journey and with learning to overcome them ... The battle does not end in the illuminative way but changes its character. A person makes progress less by directly confronting his shortcomings and sinfulness than by turning to God in deepening faith and trust. There is a shift of concern away from the need to resist sin towards the need to trust God. For he is coming to realise increasingly that God is his only strength and security.[28]

The cleansing, or purgative, way of honesty, reformation and discipline will therefore slowly and irregularly give way to a simpler but at first frightening way in which the personality is helpless even to co-operate, and the self, illumined by grace, gives itself to God. The times when this change of emphasis is happening will always be difficult, and we will often be tempted to evade them. At the beginning of this century, Poulain described the common reaction of people who had found themselves in these ineffective states but had resisted the required detachment from the ego: 'Nature inclines them to take pleasure in a distracting activity and to plunge into it to excess, were it only for the sake of escaping the tedium of their interior desert.' (Ninety years later, my own inclination at such times is to excessive television! Although, to ensure physical distraction also, it is combined with hand-sewing and at least the time is not entirely unproductive.) 'They only realize their error later on, when a book or a clear-sighted Director leads them to moderate their excesses, to reserve a larger share of their activity for their spiritual life, and not to fly from their inward purgatory.'[29]

Our part in these times of helplessness, whenever they come and however long they last, is always to hand ourselves over to God. We must, of course, have ensured that our difficulties do not arise from a return – actual, intended, or wished – to the previous sin; but if our prayers and discipline and individual methods still prove to be no use, we must take the risk of losing all that we have personally won in the loss of what God will take from us now. We are to rest against him, still frightened perhaps, but willing to be moulded by him. 'Wherefore, my beloved . . . work out your own salvation with fear and trembling. *For it is God who worketh in you both to will and to do of his good pleasure.*'[30] This is a time to suffer God's working – 'suffer', meaning both to allow and to undergo.

In *Original Blessing*, Matthew Fox describes such seemingly negative times in a way which I find particularly fitting to my own experiences of them: 'It is one thing to empty. It is an even deeper thing to be emptied. Pain does this. It empties us, if we allow it to . . . [Pain] needs to be named for what it is so that we can pray our pain, i.e., enter into it.'[31] I think that very often what we lose in these passive dark nights is the unnameable pain which we cannot give up actively because we do not know how to take hold of it, pain from the hidden wounds which only God can draw out from us. But even so, our part is essential; we do suffer him to operate upon us, and we make ourselves stay with the experience. 'Facing the darkness, admitting the pain, allowing the pain to be pain, is never easy. This is why courage – big-heartedness – is the most essential virtue on the spiritual journey. But if we fail to let pain be pain . . . then pain will haunt us in nightmarish ways.'[32] We have already known some of that nightmare, in our sin and separation, and for many of us the reason it happened at all was our total inability, as helpless infants, to 'let pain be pain'. Now in a healing darkness we are given another chance to allow the pain and the growth.

The traditional manuals of mystic prayer describe a state in which the person is given 'a simple gaze directed almost wholly towards God',[33] and is in fact unable to keep his or her sight and mind upon anything else. For such people, dedicated to a life of seclusion and devotion, this inner simplicity is a gift which they have now become capable of receiving; for us, at this stage of the struggle, there is an equivalent attitude, which we can choose to practise. Sometimes we even must choose it, if we are not to fall away disastrously. We can deliberately keep ourselves turned only in the direction of God. However much the edges of our minds may be fretted and besieged by old fears and temptations, we can hold our gaze yearning into the darkness where we know he must be, while we say the one thing which can uphold us in the emptiness – 'Only you, God. Only you. I want only you.' This is not a denial of our material setting, an escape from human relationship or daily obligations. It is a hunger for the reality of the Spirit which is within human life and activities, and a commitment to the search for it. We are ordinary people living in the world, we want to experience God within affection and sex and friendship and co-operation – but it is God's reality we want in them, not the old defences and satisfactions and substitutes we used to wring from them. Our simple, single, yearning need is for God and our goodness. 'Only you, good Lord, and my true self in you.' As the contemplative is *given* only God, so the troubled, sin-weary soul *calls for* only God, in the dark night of material, physical, emotional and psychological emptiness and strain.

**Willing to be cleansed**

I have used the words 'purging' and 'purgation' despite their unpopularity. I like the way they suggest a process in which we are cleansed of whatever is misshapen, harmful or limiting in ourselves. I see the image of a metal heated beyond its ordinary state to rid it of impurities; when cooled and reshaped and hard again, it is purged of its baser elements and more useful for its purpose. Purgation can be a searing, stripping time, but we have seen that, under one name or another, it is an essential stage of our journey.

All the early struggle against sin is an attempt to purge ourselves of the darkness and distortion which hinder that journey. Drawn by the vision of an unpolluted life, we work to cleanse ourselves, or we submit to a purification by the Spirit. An essential element in this process is our willingness to have it happen to us. 'Purgatory is the place where freedom begins to come alive in us.'[34] A great deal of wrongdoing is a sort of drift, rather than a deliberate disobedience; when we find out how difficult the life of faith can be, we hold back and reduce our efforts, and therefore slide into sin almost by default. Then when we do begin to choose something else, it is cleansing which we first have to say 'Yes' to. 'Purgation (or self-simplification) is a way of "clearing the decks for action". The house is swept and polished and the garbage is collected and burned. The purpose of purgation is always remedial and never punitive. It is meant to help and not to punish us.'[35]

Traditionally, hell is the place of punishment for absolutely disobedient and rebellious souls, but our common usage confuses the terms. 'It's hell', we say when asked how we're getting on without cigarettes, but we know it is not a punishment from somebody else who is forcing us to give them up. 'It's purgatory', we might be as likely to reply, and more accurately also, because we have chosen the process, which is one of cleansing. We have the opportunities to choose innumerable processes of purgation in our lives; and to choose purgatory after death, too, as a place or state in which to be purged of the remaining effects of sin. St Catherine of Genoa imagined a soul leaping into purgatory, eager for the further cleansing which would burn away the last barriers between itself and God. At the moment of death such a soul says one final 'Yes' and endures whatever is to come; I believe that during our lives we have the freedom to say 'Yes' over and over again, to take part with a free will and therefore with great effectiveness in our own purifying. Von Hügel was at pains to make clear the 'truly great doctrine of Purgatory' in one of his spiritual letters:

> According to that doctrine, suffering (*rightly accepted* suffering) is indeed usually necessary for, is inherent in, the Purification from sin, evil habits, etc. But it makes no substantial distinction between such Purification as taking place already here, or taking place in the Beyond . . . In all cases, Purgatory applies indifferently to suffering rightly borne in *this* life and the same similarly borne in *that* life . . . every pang which God allows to reach us here, and which we manage to bear a little well, does *a work not to be repeated*.[36]

That compassionate, moderate 'bear a little well' reminds me of Winnicott's 'good enough mothering'. We do not have to be perfect, without any hesitation, living every single line of the vision. If we just bear the suffering and the changes 'a little well', grace will carry us forward. And it really is suffering. To be hungry without our junk-food satisfactions, to endure the loss of our props and protections, to allow into consciousness the terror and desolation of our earliest wounds – this is suffering; it deserves our tears and fear. But I do know, from my own experience, that every time we truly suffer our own depths, it is a work not to be repeated. The pain *is* finite and does decrease; our strength *does* grow, and becomes more effective; the benefits *are* to be enjoyed in this life. They may often not be the ones we had looked for, but that only means we are still not looking aright at our path, our own unique personal path with its unexpected creative changes, nor understanding the new values it uncovers to us.

We can find purgatory everywhere. Nowadays many people choose it, though they might not name it so, when they go to encounter groups or enter psychotherapy. A 'self-help' group of friends sharing their spiritual journeys, a marriage submitting itself to counselling, a 'prayer sharing' circle, a new workers' co-operative – all are cleansing experiences aimed at transformation of life on some level. It is therefore right for us to choose our purgatory and to be glad of the chance. It is a time when we exercise our freedom and responsibility as co-workers with God, sharing with the Spirit the task of re-making our lives, redeeming the lost years, and transforming the future.

**Transmuting the past**

There is a particular experience we may encounter when we are transforming our lives; it is subtle, beautiful, paradoxical, nearly impossible to describe. It is the experience of changing the past. On one level this is fairly simple: by the way we live out a decision we change the apparent meaning and intention of the actions which led up to it, and which might not at the time have seemed to be leading specifically to it, at all. We create the meaning of the past in which the decision was made by the way that we decide and act in the present.

But that only boils down to a different way of looking upon the past; and I do not mean merely that because of the way we live the future we have said something about the time of decision in the past, nor even that we reveal something in the past which was not visible at the time. It is more like this: by the choice we make, we change the meaning and intention of the actions which led up to it. By the decision and the way we live forward from it, we re-create the past which was before the decision. Spiritual energy is not limited to space and time; spiritual energy which is expended now in decision and action may feed into the past before these decisions and actions were contemplated and help to bring them about. Later on we may, fleetingly, see backwards and glimpse the several paths which were unfolding at the same time and shiver to realize how vigorously we were following a wrong one, and yet how the right one we now feel so strongly was even then pulling us towards it. Or we may, in the present, sense the choices which are still to come and be subtly aware that the person we are going to be is already making its choice of them. In this paradoxical non-time it is all the more urgent for us to be aware of the energy of growth and to be responding to it from our living goodness so that the created path is truly the right one.

This is a theme which Charles Williams explored in *Descent into Hell*, but C. S. Lewis described it better than anyone else I know of. A wise old man is talking to him, in the strange landscape to which the mysterious coach has taken him:

> Both good and evil, when they are full grown, become retrospective. Not only this valley but all their earthly past will have been Heaven to those that are saved. Not only the twilight in that town, but all their life on earth too, will then be seen by the damned to have been Hell. That is what mortals misunderstand. They say of some temporal suffering, 'No future bliss can make up for it', not knowing that Heaven, once attained, will work backwards and turn even that agony into a glory. And of some sinful pleasure they say 'Let me but have *this* and I'll take the consequences': little dreaming how damnation will spread back

and back into their past and contaminate the pleasure of the sin. Both processes begin even before death. The good man's past begins to change so that his forgiven sins and remembered sorrows take on the quality of Heaven: the bad man's past already conforms to his badness and is filled only with dreariness. And that is why, at the end of all things, when the sun rises here and the twilight turns to blackness down there, the Blessed will say 'We have never lived anywhere except in Heaven', and the Lost, 'We were always in Hell'. And both will speak truly . . . Ah, the Saved . . . what happens to them is best described as the opposite of a mirage. What seemed, when they entered it, to be the vale of misery turns out, when they look back, to have been a well; and where present experience saw only salt deserts, memory truthfully records that the pools were full of water.[37]

All their created past *will have been* Heaven . . . Not 'will have become', not was one thing and is made into another, but, from this new landscape which the pilgrims' path has led into, it will have been the right place which has led to this new right place for us.

# 8

# THERE IS NO WRATH IN GOD

**Relationship without qualification**

As we travel through the letting go and losing, our changing knowledge of our personal lives needs to be supported by a wider and deeper perspective. In chapter 3 we saw how early wounds often lead to views of God which emphasize power, anger and vengeance, or at best unpredictability or indifference. We have had to be willing to let go of these images, along with so much else which has hindered our travelling. God himself helps to divest us of them, because he is always giving himself to us as he truly is, and waiting for us to be able to see the truth of him.

But we will also have to question the views of God which are presented by our communities and the organizational churches. We may have to let go of our churches, or even to resist their hold and make them let go of us. Matthew Fox is a passionate advocate of new attitudes in the churches, or outside of them if they will not change. 'To recover the wisdom that is lurking in religious traditions we have to let go of more recent religious traditions', he says. He advocates in particular a giving up of the exclusively fall/redemption model of spirituality which has dominated the churches' patriarchal and dualistic teaching for centuries. In that model, sinful humanity is the centre of the spiritual universe; in Fox's model, the starting point for spirituality is a blessed universe of grace. 'Original blessing is prior to any sin, original or less than original . . . the time has come to let anthropocentrism go, and with it to let the preoccupation with human sinfulness give way to attention to divine grace. In the process sin itself will be more fully understood and more successfully dealt with.'[1]

If one does not – and I do not – believe in an original guilty fall, then one's theology cannot end with redemption either. Both falling and redeeming are currents in the constant flow of life, and we take part in the latter just as we have been a part of the former. My dictionary says of 'redeem': 'to recover possession by payment of a price'. We have to recover ourselves, and the price is the surrender of our falseness. It continues: 'to make amends' – all our work now does that; 'to restore to favour' – but here I baulk, for I cannot believe that we need to be 'restored to favour'. We do not fall out of favour; we cannot fall out of the Love in which we have our being.

We are not loved because of what we are, nor even in spite of what we are, but just because God is Love, and he therefore must love; he has given himself no other choice. The church, any of the churches, can tell me that he is angry and punishing, but I cannot find it anywhere in my experience. Punishment and anger I have known, indeed, but they have not been God's. I know their name, and for that very reason I know it is not God's name; and throughout the centuries also there have been other voices to affirm that God's true name is Love, since it was named for us in the West two thousand years ago. 'God is love' is an unqualified and absolute statement,[2] which our preachers and teachers seem so often to have had difficulty in accepting without qualification, partly I suppose because 'love' is one of the most catch-all words in our language. It is, indeed, one of the most catch-all concepts of our experience! I like Bishop Stephen Neill's definition of agape: 'the steady directing of the . . . will towards the eternal well-being of another'.[3] Our well-being is God's will, and we share his will when we will, and work, towards the well-being of others. Love is *relating in goodness*.

I have said that 'the energy which forms and maintains relationships is Love, and the energy which formed and maintains that total relationship which we call the universe is the creative and sustaining Love of God. All relating is . . . God working.' The very atoms which make up my body would fall apart if God did not hold them in relationship to each other. 'Our Lord God cannot in his own judgement forgive, because he cannot be angry – that would be impossible', said Julian of Norwich long ago. 'For this was revealed, that our life is all founded and rooted in love, and without love we cannot live . . . if God could be angry for any time, we should neither have life nor place nor being.'[4] Our atoms would fall apart into chaos.

The limitless and utterly transcendent Godhead is the source of all relationship in the universe, and the personal God whom we experience is that loving relationship upholding each one of us. The Otherness of the Godhead is, of course, total; but so is the Nearness of the relating God, if we do not estrange ourselves from it. As the source of our being, God is always united with us. God's love is happening all the time, whether we feel it or not; Love acts even when we hinder it (or him, or her) with our sinfulness and fearful withdrawals; Love flows through us even though we insulate ourselves with substitutes and self-justifications. Truly, the only question is whether we *will* be aware or not, whether we welcome Love and co-operate and thus discover its joyfulness, or whether we turn our heads away and catch a distorted movement in the corners of our eyes and give a name from our shadows to what we seem to have seen. Wrath is a way we see God, not what he is.

**'I saw no wrath'**

Julian had her own problems with the church. She struggled for twenty years with the meaning of her revelation of the lord and his servant, trying to reconcile her vision of God's love with the judgement of the church that she must necessarily know herself a sinner, at least sometimes deserving blame and wrath, and know all her 'even-Christians' as blameworthy sinners too. Her difficulty was that she 'could not see these two in God'. Her conflict was long and severe, 'because of the higher judgement which God himself revealed to me at the same time, and therefore I had of necessity to accept it. And the lower judgement had previously been taught me in Holy Church, and therefore I could not in any way ignore the lower judgement'.[5] We can be enormously grateful that in her integrity Julian had to state the truth which her self had received from God: 'I saw no kind of wrath in God, neither briefly nor for long.'[6] Given her time and circumstances, it is hardly surprising that she also had to placate the church: 'And now I submit myself to my mother, Holy Church, as a simple child should'![7] How we can sympathize with her, in her struggle between the two ethics.

Once covered by that disclaimer, Julian could not restrain her joyous delight at God's loving goodness and acceptance as they had been shown and given to her. She expresses it again and again in these chapters; and marvellous psychologist that she is, she sees the truth long before psychoanalysts provided the concept of projecting our distortions onto other people and onto God:

> For I saw no wrath except on man's side, and he forgives that in us, for wrath is nothing else but a perversity and an opposition to peace and to love. And it comes from a lack of power or a lack of wisdom or a lack of goodness, and this lack is not in God, but it is on our side.[8]

We see our own hobgoblins and shadows, and say that they are God.

I have to wonder what the preachers and teachers have been getting out of their emphasis upon God's wrath, throughout the centuries. It is not a necessary part of Christian faith; it is not what Jesus said about his Father. All my dictionaries define wrath as in some way violent and vengeful; and indeed many fathers are, and that is what many of us learn about fathers, or mothers, but it is not what he said about that Father. And long before him, Jeremiah was shown the Lord anew: 'Let him that glorieth glory in this, that he understandeth and knoweth me, that I am the Lord which exercise loving kindness, judgement, and righteousness, in the earth: for in these things I delight, saith the Lord.'[9] Admittedly, in the Old Testament context of

'I will punish them' it was perhaps not unreasonable to read 'wrath' into judgement and righteousness, but it is not essential. We all exercise judgement when we decide whether something is right or wrong, in order to know whether to do it, or take part in it, or respond to it: we could not expect God to do less. And as for righteousness – well, if it were taken to mean 'honouring the path of what is right' rather than 'self-righteousness', surely all pilgrims desire it? Neither judgement nor righteousness are necessarily wrathful.

Throughout the centuries there have also been voices, too rarely echoed in the formal doctrine of the churches, to agree with Jeremiah and Jesus and Julian. In the sixteenth century the Lutheran mystic Jacob Boehme wrote, 'Reason says that because man was found disobedient God cast His fierce anger upon him . . . Thou must not think such thoughts. For God is love and goodness, and there is not one angry thought in Him.' A hundred-plus years later, the stubborn but moderate Anglican William Law was unusually emphatic: 'From eternity to eternity no spark of wrath ever was or ever will be in the holy triune God.'[10]

Evidence for the antiquity of the struggle between the two ethics can be found in a most respectable source. Richard Moulton, in his *Modern Reader's Bible*, refers to the recognition of Jeremiah as the central point in the history of his people 'where the overthrow of a national religion becomes the starting point for the religion of the individual life and the "new covenant" written on the heart', and he translates the prophet thus:

> 'But this is the covenant that I will make with the house of Israel . . . I will put my law in their inward parts, and in their hearts will I write it; and I will be their God, and they shall be my people: and they shall teach no more every man his neighbour, and every man his brother, saying, Know the Lord: for they shall all know me, from the least of them unto the greatest of them, saith the Lord.'[11]

We shall all know him, and from our explorers' experience we will decide whether ours is to be a theology of wrath or of love. Charles Williams, the lay theologian, poet, critic, and 'mystic' novelist, is a modern explorer and prophet who offers us a vision of this universal doctrine, shared rather than taught, and practised in the

> restoration of humility, of sanctity, of joy . . . The law that is to be written within is to be written everywhere: instinctive as the heart, broad as the earth . . . All evil is to be forgotten. Within and without, present and past, the world is to know good as good, and to practise it between themselves.[12]

I believe that we cannot practise good between ourselves if we perceive wrath in God. Such a perception in itself points to the wrath or fear of wrath in us, which God will take from our hearts if we will let go of it. Before that can happen, we must realize that the wrath *is* in us; and if my explanation and Julian's glowing vision and Jeremiah's new covenant have not persuaded you, perhaps Williams' wry humour will prove irresistible. In *The Forgiveness of Sins* he presents a delightful challenge to the idea that God was 'offended' by the disobedience of Adam and Eve. Can that divine Other be credited with either our virtues or our vices? Can he, very strictly speaking, be 'angry' at all?

> He laid commandments on us; we disobey; very well, is he to be angry? Obviously not, unless he chooses that he shall; all his motions are his will. If one created (if one could and dared) two blackbeetles, and bade them copulate only on Tuesday and they did it on Thursday, would one be 'angry' with them unless one chose? Make the command as rational as one can; suppose one had made them only capable of happy copulation once in seven days, and they hurt themselves by disobedience – even then, would one be *angry*? Still less, he; unless indeed it is supposed to be part of his nature to permit himself the infinite indulgence of superior spite.[13]

Do *you* think that God indulges in superior spite?

William Law said that 'there is no wrath that stands between

God and us but what is awakened in the dark fire of our own fallen nature . . . And this wrath which may be called the wrath of God is not God, but is the fiery wrath of the fallen soul.'[14] It may be in our own souls, that fury and retaliation and unforgivingness; but it may also be what we learned in the veiled or open wrath we suffered before we had a name for it, or in the names we have heard in our schools and churches. It may not be 'mine' in the sense that I as an individual am responsible for having it, but it is 'ours', humankind's ungovernable anger expended upon anyone nearby: enemy, refugee, Jew, infant, black man, wife – or God. Many will remain torn between their hope that there is no wrath in God, and the family/society/church insistence that there is; many more will have internalized the wrath they have suffered from and will 'know' that is how the universe is, or will have projected their own actual rage onto God whom they cannot see in any other way. Whether victim or perpetrator, or victim/perpetrator, they suffer from 'an incomplete possession by the spirit of love'.[15] We need to allow the fullest possession of ourselves by this spirit of Love, flowing into the creeks and marshes of our wounded nature, so that our sight is cleansed and we no longer mistake what is there to be seen when we look Godwards.

**The searing gaze of love**

We cannot resist some possession by the spirit of Love, for a part of us is always vulnerable to it. But the possession will be incomplete if we block it with old ideas and attitudes, avoid the claims it will make upon us, or hold back from the changes which it will bring. Especially when we are in sin, whether we have chosen it freely or have been driven to it by fear, we do not – we dare not – allow Love to enter the dark corners of our egos. We know, though we have refused to admit, what sorts of things it will find there.

But when compunction has opened our hearts and we no longer forbid Love's entrance, it exposes our sin and makes us feel the full pain of our separation. Its purpose is not to cause pain or shame, it simply shines upon what we have really done and what we have become, but now we share with it the unblurred sight of the effects of sin, and are appalled. *The wrath of God is the spirit of Love exposing the estrangement of sin.* It is Love which gazes, lovingly, and not wrath, vengefully, but its uncompromising purity sears us to the core. Julian knew it, as she knew so much: '. . . he touches us most secretly, and shows us our sins by the sweet light of mercy and grace. But when we see ourselves so foul, then we may believe that God may be angry with us because of our sins.'[16] Because Love is Reality, pure and whole, its gaze penetrates all disguises and defences. Laser-like, it ignores our bandages, and that hurts. We recoil and resist and rebel; no wonder it seems like punishment. 'Love takes off the masks that we fear we cannot live without and know we cannot live within.'[17]

There is undoubtedly an experience which has been called (however inaccurately in my opinion) 'feeling the wrath of God'. Knowing our sin, we are ashamed, guilty, fearing a dreadful punishment, wishing we could escape whatever will happen. It is entirely natural for us to expect wrath and to interpret our feelings as being the result of well deserved wrath. But if we look afresh at this experience, without old explanations and opinions, we can see the possibility that we have mistaken simple cause and effect for punitive venom. For every action there is an equal and opposite reaction – God's uncompromising gaze upon our estrangement is the action, and react we must. But this can be the instinctive reaction of fearing and resisting wrath, or the chosen one of opening to the agony of love. Our sin separates us from God – that is cause and effect; his truth exposes our separation – inevitable effect. But in our fearfulness and immaturity we interpret this exposure as *his* punishment instead of the consequences of *our* self-isolating sin. 'The punishment, the pain or the hell of sin is no designedly prepared or arbitrary penalty inflicted by God, but the natural and necessary state of the creature that leaves or turns from God.'[18]

The experience of looking at our own sin without excuses and justifications is one of turning again to God, of partaking in his gaze, of seeing sin piercingly. If we resent or fear that gaze, we will experience God as vengeful and furious, and will be thrown back into a hall of mirrors where we cannot see anything realistically. If we welcome the truth at last just because it is the truth and we need it, then we will feel the love and forgiveness which is the gaze of God and will know that there is no anger or blame in it. Like the pain of acceptance which takes away our reasons for avoiding self-knowledge, the pain of this loving gaze offers us one of the most precious but most difficult gifts in life: reality.

So the wrath is in us, not in God. It is our own fear of punishment, our recoil from truth, our unwillingness to be responsible – our sheer cold terror of reality. We are afraid to know that if we open to it, love is a healing cautery. However mysteriously negative the Godhead may be, the God of loving relationship cannot be wrathful – it is a contradiction of terms. Even if there is some inconceivable form of wrath in the 'hidden God', that negativity is overcome or absorbed by the God of relating love as he reaches across separation to us. He accepts always: it is we who flee acceptance and perceive anger where there is none.

## Melting the ice block

Perhaps some of the pain and vulnerability of being accepted lies in its being a one-way action, in which we have a limited part and which we cannot very much influence. Acceptance is taking what is offered, but it is not *exchange*. It is not, in itself, dynamic, and therefore does not carry us – either as an idea or an experience – far enough. The Unitarian minister Joy Croft said:

> The whole concept of sin, and certainly of guilt, suggests something which persists through time and which you *drag* around with you, as opposed to things like love and anger, which are very much alive and happen by living in the moment. It is forgiveness which breaks up the log jam, turning something which is solid, and dry, and weighty, and enduring, into something which flows again. Forgive-

ness has that sort of power in a way that just acceptance doesn't.[19]

Acceptance takes the situation as it is, without rancour or blame indeed, but also without the energy to 'break up the log jam', whereas forgiveness changes the situation, makes it live again and grow. In a sermon on forgiveness, Joy retold the Hans Christian Andersen story of the Snow Queen. In it, the children Kay and Gerda have lived in gentle love towards each other until the Evil One breaks his evil, distorting mirror, and a fragment lodges in Kay's eye so that he now sees the beautiful as ugly, and ugliness as beauty. To him, even the freezing Snow Queen is beautiful, and he follows her to the Ice Palace. There he moves blocks of ice back and forth to form letters, and the Snow Queen tells him that if he can use them to spell that 'long cold word, eternity', she will give him 'the whole world and a pair of skates'. But she does not offer him his freedom, and Kay is a long way from discovering it in himself, for the sliver of ice mirror has worked its way down to his heart and frozen it, and he cannot even remember the warmth and loveliness of life.

A lot of our feelings, Joy Croft says, have active and flowing states and also hard and frozen states without any energy of movement. Swift, alerting fear may become solidified into anxiety which prevents the necessary saving reaction; love, the most creative of emotions, can harden into the sort of blind loyalty which does not grow with the changing situation. Anger can be a vibrant quality which helps us to change what has gone wrong, but if it is not expressed it can become frozen into hate, or the milder form, resentment. These blocked and hardened emotions are like Kay's ice blocks, and the ice mirror: we cannot see through them to the other person as he or she really is and to what there can be between us, but only see ourselves reflected in them, distortingly. We get caught in frozen situations which will not change or grow. Guilt, too, despite its torments, is a solidified state, until compunction turns it into flowing remorse and redeeming action.

When at last Gerda finds Kay in the Ice Palace, sadly wrestling with the blocks of ice which will not form lovely words, her heart aches for him and she does not care that he ran away and that she has suffered many dangers in her search for him. She hugs him, and her warm, forgiving tears melt his heart so that his feelings too begin to flow and he cries so hard that even the fragment of the ice mirror is washed out of his eye. He is able to love Gerda again, and they leave the Ice Palace together. It was her forgiving love which freed him. Forgiveness has the power to thaw hate and resentment, guilt and fear, which lie across the path of our relationships like unyielding blocks.

God's gaze, which sears our guilt, is a gaze of forgiving warmth when we endure it. He does not merely gaze, staying over there somewhere and looking at us from a distance, however lovingly. He relates. He reaches out to us with open arms. Like Gerda, he moves towards and with us, and wants us to move with him. Life with God is a flowing outwards from the springs of forgiveness, and to share it we need to do more than just accept his gaze and its reality – we need to take part in the forgiveness.

## Bridging the divide

Forgiveness is basically the renewing of a relationship which has been broken by harm and wrong. A harm done by one person to another breaks the loving link between them, and forgiveness restores that link. Love overcomes or absorbs the wrong on all its levels, and reaches across the separation which it had caused. Forgiveness is different from pardon, which emphasizes the removal of the consequences of the fault or damage. If a friend defrauds me and I am suing for restitution, I may be persuaded to pardon him – then I would decide not to take the case to court, and would inform my solicitors and my bank; but I could also refuse ever to see him again, and it would still be pardon. However, it would not be forgiveness, for the friendship is broken and I will not restore it.

It is this quality of restoration which makes forgiveness so painful, and risky. Whatever the harm was, we have to know it and feel it. It cannot just be locked away, or ignored, or wished out of existence. It has to be lived through, and this may be enormously painful. The man or woman who truly forgives a partner's infidelity has allowed all the feelings of betrayal and of being rejected, the anger and self-doubt, and is able to let go of them, so that the restoration of the relationship will be complete. That does not have to mean that they are meekly swallowed. 'You have hurt me badly', she can say. 'I've been angry and disgusted, and that was hard to deal with. But I want you to come back, because I love you and I think what we've got is valuable and worth working for.' She says: I forgive you; but she also names what it is she has had to forgive.

And she takes the risk that it will happen again, or something like it, or something else which will hurt just as much. We can say 'I forgive you, and I hope you will not do it again', because we have the right to want not to be hurt and betrayed. But we cannot say 'If you promise not to do it again, I will forgive you', for that is buying compliance, not renewing a broken relationship of love. Love is always the taking of a risk on another person: forgiveness is love which has learned a bit more about the risks.

But it can happen that the person who has been injured does not need to forgive. 'That's all right,' we may say about some minor issue, 'there's nothing to forgive.' We do not mean that nothing happened, but that it was not enough to damage our love and care. We are not depreciating our friend's remorse and shame, but are telling him or her that it can be put aside, because there is still love between us to be shared, and we have not been separated by what was done. This may be true even of a very great injury. The deeper and sturdier and more enduring our love for another is, the greater the injury we can receive without that love being broken by it. The heartache and horror and indignation are very real and have to be dealt with, but they are like a dislocation to a joint or a deep flesh wound, and beneath them the heartbeat and the blood-flow of love continue, sustaining the relationship and then healing the injury to it, but not having to overcome a break in it. If the person who was harmed did not break the ties with the other in the first reaction of pain, or does not find that they have been broken despite all the goodwill and charity which tried to hold them intact, then he or she does not have to *forgive* but merely *continues to love*.

Sometimes, perhaps often, forgiveness is a necessary act not for the person who has been injured, but in order to assure the wrongdoer that the relationship is indeed not broken. It is not a restoration at all, but an affirmation. 'If you need to know that love remains unbroken, and will be assured of that by words of forgiveness, then you have them, willingly; but I don't need to forgive, because what you did to me didn't break my loving feeling for you.' In this case, the words of forgiveness are usually a tender formality, a way to draw the friend, or lover, or colleague, or child back into the ambit of exchange and to take up the threads of life together again. But it may turn out to be a challenge for the one who asked for forgiveness. If there had been some harmful intention in what was done, it will not be enough just to regret the act. The attitudes and desires which led to it will have to be looked at and admitted, however privately, and then be given up so that the relationship can flow and grow as it should.

Being forgiven thaws our guilt, undoes the knots of blame and self-blame, and enables us to return to the relationship which is waiting for us. In our relationship with God, he is *always* waiting and always reaching out to us. He never stops being present in grace, whether or not we are able to see or to feel that presence. 'For our courteous Lord does not want his servants to despair because they fall often and grievously; for our falling does not hinder him in loving us. Peace and love are always in us, living and working, but we are not always in peace and love.'[20] That unbroken offering of love is continuous forgiveness. When Jesus said, 'Your sins are forgiven', he seemed to say, 'What you have to do now is to live your side of it'. Our part is to accept forgiveness and take up the responsibilities which that brings.

Julian of Norwich saw, to her astonishment, 'our Lord God showing no more blame to us than if we were as pure and holy as the angels are in heaven'.[21] 'Though it may be that we act like this often, his goodness never allows us to be alone, but constantly he is with us, and tenderly he excuses us, and always protects us from blame in his sight.'²² Clearly, God does not see sin the same way we do. He looks at us from the other side of sin, from within love. Even in human affairs, as I have said, there are times when love is not broken by harm. The closer one dwells to the centre of love, the more true it is that hurtful things seem to happen superficially to love. Therefore, really – that is, in the fullness of Reality – they have not happened at all, as though a person who lived high among alpine meadows was undisturbed by flooding in the valleys far below. If we could live at the centre, the goodness and the love which are always here with us would matter very much more than the wrong and the sin which are done to us time and time again but, so to speak, down there, in the turmoil of the flooded plain. I do not mean to suggest something rarefied and unearthly. I am talking about situations where a person will have been materially harmed by another, and have suffered emotionally, but even so the self of that person and its lovingness remain whole and undamaged. Since we humans are able to do this sometimes, we can see how God could be doing it all the time. In a way similar to what we sometimes manage, but to an almost unimaginable degree, he remains unbroken from himself, and his love unbroken from us. In the Old Testament, God speaks through Isaiah with a great tenderness: 'I . . . am he that blotteth out thy transgressions . . . and will not remember thy sins. Put me in remembrance: let us plead together.'²³ Charles Williams writes:

> In the great healing and restoration which he has promised, the High and Holy One will set aside even the memory of sin. This depends certainly on Israel's repentance; but once that is in process, the past is to be remembered no more. 'Behold, I create new heavens and a new earth: and the former shall not be remembered nor come into mind.'²⁴

For Christians, Christ is the form in which God made his restoration of broken relationship, the unique and essential form who was atonement for sins. Even for post-Christians or non-Christians, 'Christ' can be one of the names for this action by

God. Certainly, as Jesus and scripture and the churches have claimed and we can experience, God does do it; he does it in his eternal nature, in eternity, and therefore for us in time he always has and always will do it. The churches say, 'God's broken love is restored – by Christ', which is really to say, if Christ and God are one, 'God's broken love is restored by himself', and even more, that the break and the restoration are co-existent and perpetual. Since love is happening all the time, forgiveness is also happening all the time.

But I, and others, say something further: God does not even allow his love to be broken; he 'blotteth out our transgressions', they do not even exist. Love and forgiveness are certainly synchronous in God, and more than that, they are synonymous. But the change which has to happen is our recognition of this truth. It is we who are separated from God, and when we have stopped doing what separates us then we can look with fresh eyes and hearts at the unbroken love which is always offered to us. Many of us are comfortless in churches which fail to convince us of the unbroken relationship we can always return to, or to help us restore the break in love which undoubtedly occurs on our side. We need to achieve our return to that relationship by our own recognition of this truth, and our own reminder to ourselves of our true nature. William Law reminds us that the true forgiveness of sins is a new birth of the divine life in us, for the sinful state is 'nothing else but the loss of that divine nature which cannot commit sin; therefore, the forgiving man's sin is, in the truth and reality of it, nothing else but the revival of that nature in man which, being born of God, sinneth not.'[25]

## Accepting forgiveness, and giving it

We could even say that the experience of God's forgiveness is not of something particular which God does, but is feeling our acceptance of what he is always doing and our response to it. Having been blinded by our separation in sin, we see at last that we are loved and we call this seeing 'being forgiven'. We cannot do it unless we look at him, we cannot look while we are caught in our sin, and we are caught until we let go of it. But grace continually brings opportunities to realize what we are doing, it opens our hearts to repentance and strengthens our determination to live by other values. It is grace working in us which kindles our courage to be forgiven. God always wants us to be reunited with him, and at last our own desire for it becomes effective. The acceptance of forgiveness is a warm-hearted and full-hearted willingness to take part again in the life of grace.

As we share in God's work, so he asks us to share in forgiveness by forgiving ourselves for the break in our own lovingness. We cannot even recognize God's forgiveness unless we have forgiven ourselves, and have melted the ice block which held us immobile. It is largely the persistent sense of guilt and unworthiness which cuts us off from God within us, so that it could be said that the failure to forgive ourselves would be one of the primary sins! It would unnecessarily perpetuate the hurtful separation. Therefore, once we have admitted the wrong and harm we have done, we too must 'blot out our transgressions', and move on; it would be wrong to dwell any longer on the previous sin or guilt. We must remember the message from it, of course, remember and use what we learned from it and from repentance, but do so as a reason to go forward into a different life. Kazoh Kitamori writes of the pain of being a forgiver: 'However, the pain, if real, penetrates the one who forgives, and issues forth in intent love . . . Forgiveness exhibits its true nature, and pain proves to be real, only when intent love enfolds others, forgetting its pain.'[26] It is often just as painful to forgive ourselves, and at least as important to accept the pain of it, the shame and vulnerability and challenge of it. We have really forgiven ourselves when we allow ourselves to be enfolded in that intent love, forgetting our pain and moving into our responsibility for a truer life.

Matthew Fox writes: 'Self-forgiveness is a great spiritual gift. We ought to pass it on wherever possible, whether as parent or as sisters and brothers, friends or enemies. One of the greatest helps in learning self-forgiveness is learning the truth of God's forgiveness. For it is everywhere.'[27]

But we must not think that having been forgiven (whether by God, ourselves, or those we have harmed) is an easy condition. When we at last accept God's forgiveness, we realize that the spiritual slate has always been clean, we see the part of ourselves which never assented to sin. This is where we can centre, where we can find our new values and from which we can live; but we must also, so to speak, clean the psychological, personal and material slates. We have to live through the consequences of sin on all these other levels. There will be external consequences to be made good or endured, and sometimes long remorse because we cannot make them good. There will be personality characteristics and deeply ingrained habits of living to resist and slowly change. Whatever we gained from sinning will have to be given up, and it may be a long time before we discover the benefits of this long and sometimes bewildering transformation. So forgiveness is not an escape from consequences; but the difference now is that they can be lived through from a different position – from within the knowledge that there is an undying goodness within us to seek, and hold to, and express. Through this painful response to forgiveness, we grow out of being just 'stumps of men'.

Our forgiveness of others is also born in this revealed centre of goodness, and is just as painful and difficult in its own way. In chapter 3 we examined some of the terrible damage which can be done to us in our earliest months and years. When we travel the path of self-knowledge and explore these painful areas, we have to learn both rightful accusation and willing forgiveness. Fox goes on to say that the prophets preached the freedom which forgiveness brings:

> The 'broken-hearted and the crushed in spirit' are both forgiven and freed . . . Their forgiveness and freedom is [also] related to forgiving in the sense of undoing the sins of those who oppress them. Not to forgive is to put in motion a spiral of oppression and sin . . . Others need forgiveness as much and often more than we; and in that forgiveness lies our own releasement.[28]

Probably we cannot succeed in blotting out their transgressions, but certainly we need to take the old pain into ourselves consciously, and to renew, or sometimes even to develop for the first time, our loving movement towards them. It may be that in current still-troubled relationships we are not able to express this very openly, and if those who injured us are now dead the love can only live quietly in us, without even any direct expression of it; but it is essential for us nevertheless. We received hatred from them, or other harm so dreadful that we could not have distinguished it from hate, but to let hate live on in us would only harm us further. Martin Luther King asked why we should love our enemies and gave a characteristically beautiful and powerful reason:

> Returning hate for hate multiplies hate, adding deeper darkness to a night already devoid of stars. Darkness cannot drive out darkness; only light can do that. Hate cannot drive out hate; only love can do that . . . Hate scars the soul and distorts the personality. Mindful that hate is an evil and dangerous force, we too often think of what it does to the person hated . . . [but] hate is just as injurious to the person who hates. Like an unchecked cancer, hate corrodes the personality and eats away its vital unity.[29]

As very faulty human beings, *we* cannot be without wrath; and indeed it would not be good to try. But we can come to understand our anger, to distinguish between that which is only defensive or even retaliatory and that which is justified and is actually right for us to feel and to use. Alice Miller, in her splendid championing of the damaged child, stresses the importance of an 'enlightened witness'[30] whose living testimony is so important to the liberation of anyone who has been abused. For her, as a therapist, the witness will usually be a therapist; but she also speaks of the value of such a witness during childhood. This will be someone the child encountered then who was not cruel, and will thus enable him or her to make a comparison with the parents' behaviour and to recognize its cruelty.

For us, on the path we are sharing in this book, God is the 'enlightened witness', even if others fail or were never there at all. He is most intimately present to all our pain and anger, and most reliably uncompromising towards all the false names which others, or even we ourselves, try to give to what happened and sometimes is still happening. When I at last named the truth of what had been done to me, it was with the words, 'Here I stand, God's righteous law at my back, and say, "What you did to me was wrong".' There was no other witness for me to call upon; but this one did not fail me. Slowly but steadily my girlhood repudiation of hatred and bitterness as a solution to life's problems grew into a mature, positive willingness and ability to face what had been done, to acknowledge its scars, to examine, judge, and at last to forgive with compassion and relief.

Awareness of God with us in our search helps us to face our truth prayerfully and in trust that it will come out of the shadows only as our strength can deal with it. And our awareness of God with us will also draw us into that further step of forgiveness.

# 9

## THE PAIN OF GOD

**The cost of forgiveness**

It is not easy to put aside harm which has been done: it is costly and painful both for the one who sins and the one who forgives. But the harm of our sin has to be *made not to matter*, be put out of attention even if it cannot be put entirely out of mind, because there is something else to turn to which is infinitely more important. Even in human affairs, when once the damage we suffered is understood and responsibility for it has been assigned, when our true guilt is distinguished from our burden of unjustified guilt and has been accepted, and heart-aching compunction has started us on the necessary changes in what we do, then reconciled relationship for the future has to matter more than anything in the past. In our separation from God, beyond the harm which we have done to ourselves is the new relationship with him. And beyond the harm which our separation has done in the universe of relationship is God's overarching love and healing, the new centre of our attention and aspiration.

Together, in this book, we have felt the aching fearfulness of that separation, and the need for it to be overcome. We have considered the pain which we must accept if we are to let go of our sin, of its protection and its gains. We have looked at the anguish which was caused by the searing light of truth. We know what the road to forgiveness has cost us.

What does it cost God? Our own experience guides us to an answer. In *The Pain of Christ*, Gerald Vann says, 'Let us learn of human love as a parable.'[1] Human love must be an abysmally inadequate image of God's love, but it is the only guide we have. If we look at the best we can possibly imagine of love and forgiveness, and then send our imagination leaping beyond even that, perhaps we can begin to understand his loving. Imagine, for example (or perhaps, sadly, remember) some situation where you have been greatly wronged by someone you love, your trust betrayed, harm done both to you and to the relationship which it will take a lot of effort to put right. But you do still love, and that pain tears you apart. The imperative to overcome the harm for the sake of the love tears you apart.

> When our fellow becomes an 'enemy' who betrays our love, and we continue to love him still more deeply, then pain is born in us. In an ethic without pain we love our fellow only as long as he is worthy of our love; then, when he is no longer worthy, we drop him and forget him. There is no constancy in such a love . . . [But] love of the unlovable, when we are absolutely consistent in it, displays the power to transform the unlovable into the *lovable*. This is *sanctification*.[2]

This is becoming like God, loving as he does – and therefore understanding more of his immutable love.

Our wrongdoing and sin, in both attitude and in specific acts, caused our separation from God: God's love has reached across this break to us who are broken away, so that the relationship shall not be broken. In this reaching out, his love fully experiences, in a way we can barely comprehend, the rejection and refusal of the sinner, the rending disjunction in the fabric of his universe of love. Although God promised to blot out our sins, he does not 'forget' in the usual sense of the term. Omniscience has to know what has been done, and 'always' will, but he loves the repentant sinner just as though it had not been done, loves fully, openly and graciously. The knowledge of the sin, of the denial and refusal, remains in him fully, alongside the full love. That is the pain of God.

Can you feel it? Can you catch some feeling glimpse of it? God is present when we sin, present in us and with us, present in all his universe which suffers the consequences of our sin. He experiences all of it, the rejection, abuse and betrayal; he experiences in his own body which is the material creation all of the hurt and harm, the child's heartbreak, the animal's terror, the caustic pollution of the earth's green mantle. He cannot *not* suffer it because he is wholly present to it as to everything. This is the pain of the creating and relating God – that the spiritual and material universe which he is is torn awry, and he cannot escape knowing it because he experiences its whole extent and its innermost being. And *his* being pervades that pain, his love reaches all the way through it to heal the breaking which sin would have caused, before it could even happen. Some 'where', in the limitless Godhead beyond our comprehension, all is well; but in God who is our relating and generous Lord all our sins happen, and that is not well at all.

But – how can I make such a double movement clear in a sequence of words, when it is something even more than simultaneous, it is closer to one movement? – there is also God's outbreathing. 'God is that deep-rooted pain in the Universe from which love grows.'[3] The union between God and his creation cannot really be broken, because it is a union of love. Nothing, not even sin, can break love (though it can truly hide love from us). When humankind separates itself from God, then God reaches across that separation in this particular way, to maintain the union, the universe of Love. Suffering all that is done, even while he is suffering it, God reaches to us in an outpouring of love. The very extent of his pain is the measure of his love, for in order to fulfil his own nature he must fill, to the last atom, the separation which sin makes, so that there shall not be separation nor sin, but something resembling, or reflecting, all that is well. Love pours out upon us; and can you begin to imagine the anguish of that divine heart which at every moment of its loving, is also enduring our wilful rejection? This is the real meaning of the essence of forgiveness – not just the renewal of a broken relationship, but the refusal ever to let it be broken in the first place.

This, therefore, is one of the unexpected consequences of sin – when we truly face and feel the pain of our separation from

God, we are given an experience analogous to his with us, for we are reaching out to him in love and need even while we still feel the consequences of our sin, we are trying to forgive and love ourselves even as we see more and more clearly the horror of what we have done, and we are struggling to understand and love those who have hurt us, and who perhaps still do so. It is one of the paradoxes of sin which we can only appreciate when we have given it up, that it has scoured us deeply so that in our emptiness we discover greater, and sadder, depths of love. We have the chance to welcome its more-than-merely-human quality, its splendour, demand and creativity, its capacity to be an earthquake in human lives. Gerald Vann calls love the 'will-to-share'; not just the need or wish or hope, but the will, so that it does happen, whatever the situation. It is the 'will to be a *companion*',[4] in joy or pain: and it often will be in pain, for pain is a certainty. One of the most far-reaching and momentous changes in our lives is the realization of love-within-pain, and the ability to live the love because we agree to live the pain. A whole new depth of living opens to us then. There is a much deeper understanding of God in our lives, and a growing degree of gratitude for that strange, often unwelcome, but potent grace: pain-which-harbours-love.

> When the pain of God loves the human condition, it first makes human pain its own, becomes one with it, becomes immanent in it, and then seeks to resolve the pain which is tangible . . . But since the true nature of human pain is to be found *beyond* the tangible suffering, the pain of God now transcends human pain and loves it in a way that embraces and supports its very roots.[5]

Christians recognize this companionship in the immanent Christ, and I have spoken of grace entering and supporting us so that we may face our sin. Our tangible pain of sin is resolved in the tangible acts of repentance and reparation, but beyond that we realize the deeper pain of our human condition – broken, frightened and angry, hurt beyond our own healing, ill-intentioned beyond understanding. The roots of sin cannot be extricated from the roots of pain, and often we cannot tell one from the other. Their intertwined hurt is our inner condition. This is how deep the transformation must reach, this is what we must offer to God. It may be offered in certainty of love, in expectation of forgiveness, or even in lingering fear of wrath; *but nothing less than the deepest inner condition should be offered to God, and his most deeply transforming love-in-pain accepted.* When our deepest pain of estrangement, with all its elements of self-hatred, desperation and revolt, are offered to God in helpless need, he takes it into himself, absorbing it into his own pain which has longed for us in our sin, and he enters into us in the fullest, unimaginable awareness of our pain and of our need for him. We realize then that this love of his, which has never blamed us but has only grieved over us and longed for us, can carry all our pain and rebellion, carries us in all desolation, embraces and supports us always and in everything.

## A witness to the pain of God

Kazoh Kitamori's *Theology of the Pain of God*, from which I have just quoted, was the first book to crystallize for me the ideas which had grown directly out of my experience but which I had not been able to formulate. Since my earliest childhood, mine had been what I call a 'cantilevering' love, reaching out in great but ignorant effort, seventy, eighty, eighty-five per cent of the way across the divide between myself and those I needed. 'If they will not love,' was my wordless reasoning, 'then I must, so that at least there will be love in my situation.' As I matured, this egocentric emphasis changed. I became more aware of the other people as individuals, of their weaknesses and needs and the reasons why they did what they did. I began to feel the pain of knowing that they could not, in some cases would not, love me as I needed, and of continuing to love them nevertheless. I was no longer cantilevered, and longing for the response which would reach back to meet me; but I did not yet understand the pain which began to strengthen my own transformed reaching out. Then I found, by chance or grace, this little book, and responded immediately to the title.

Writing immediately after the atomic bomb devastated Hiroshima, Kitamori had terrible experience of tangible pain, but he drew also upon the long Japanese Buddhist tradition to bring a new and precise insight to the Christian mysteries of love and pain. The dry passion of the man, pressing through the maze of biblical quotations and theological technicalities, set my spirit alight:

> We dare to speak about this 'pain of God', for, to use Calvin's words, 'God does not express his great love for us in any other way'! . . . We must pronounce the words 'pain of God' as if we are allowed to speak them only once in our lifetime. Those who have beheld the pain of God cease to be loquacious, and open their mouths only by the passion to bear witness to it.
>
> Those who have seen the pain of God can live without dying, because the 'pain' is at once 'love'. By this 'love', man's pain is purified and becomes like God's 'pain'.
>
> 'Love rooted in the pain of God' cannot be observed objectively outside of our human experience. There is no way to see it other than experiencing it in our own life.[6]

And I, faulty human analogue of God, share that passion and the need to witness, out of my own small life.

Kitamori says that God's immediate love – his direct love unmediated through any form or experience, which Kitamori calls simply *the* 'love of God' – is different from the 'pain of God'. Since we are very faulty and almost always sin, in attitude if not always in actions, we constantly go against that imperative, and if the law were all, we could not experience the unmediated love as anything but wrath. To use my terms, we would experience the searing gaze without any mercy, the truth without amelioration. But the Law and the wrath of the Law are not what God offers us, for he mediates his love in pain. From his unmediated, direct love which we cannot endure in its purity grows his yearning pain for us, and from that grows the tender love which enfolds us when we welcome it. It is his pain which reaches out to us; and though it cannot reach all the way into us unless we are willing to accept it, what is there for us to accept is indeed 'God's-love-rooted-in-the-pain-of-God'.

There cannot be any more faithful love, for it knows us completely, knows and endures all our rejection, in grieving pain sustains us nonetheless, and is always ready to embrace us again when we return to it.

*God* cannot escape the experience of his own 'wrath' — that is, his own searing knowledge of the truth — because he cannot help seeing all that we do and intend; and if our hearts are too tight and small to accept a love which is rooted in pain, wrath may be all that our fearfulness will acknowledge. However, just as God eternally sees our sin but reaches out with his pain, so we, at any moment of our sin, can accept his love-in-pain, the stern tenderness which is the mediated love of God, and which Jesus revealed. Stern, because it cannot pretend that we have not sinned; tender, because it longs for our return above all else. As Kitamori says (and it must be unravelled phrase by phrase!),

> The 'love of the cross' is poured upon those turning against God's immediate love which functions as law. The 'pain of God' — the gospel — is love which is witnessed to, yet revealed, outside of the law. Both the 'pain of God' and 'love of the cross' reflect love which is poured on us by *cancelling* our sin of *rejecting* God's love.[7]

Men and women can, and do, turn against the immediate love of God, which is the law; but there is no way in which they can effectively turn against his pain-which-is-rooted-in-love, which is poured out unceasingly, because this love simply refuses to accept that rejection. It expands immeasurably, if need be, to overlap all rejection and to close the separations which we persistently produce.

Kitamori describes how the prophets sought God's wrath, the naked truth of his imperative, and the people demanded of them that it be revealed. But neither they nor we seek the wrath in itself. He says, cryptically, 'We seek God's wrath which creates man's pain in order that we may witness to the pain of God.' That is, we seek (if we truly want to overcome the separation which burdens us) the truth about what we have done so that its cleansing pain transforms us and makes us able to witness to the pain of God which we discover is his 'love-rooted-in-pain'. We bear this witness in the way we are truthful about our sin, and loving towards ourselves as sinners, and towards others with a new quality of loving. 'We must always witness to the pain of God. Man's pain as a symbol must always be on hand.'[8] When God's truth makes manifest our sin and its estrangement, we realize his pain, and the love rooted in his pain becomes a healing reality for us. Right to our depths, we must always keep in our minds, keep our hearts open to, and share, the terrible pain of estrangement which God feels, which the fabric of the universe suffers, which cripples our society. Awareness of that pain is the beginning of *our* love-rooted-in-pain which helps to mend the torn fabric of life.

When we are within sin, we are estranged from God; but when we admit to our sin we feel the pain of it, and when we long to overcome the separation we experience love-rooted-in-pain. The union which we have with God – and remember that it is not some future union, but one which we do have now, though in our sin and blindness we may not know it – is assured by the pain of God, that is, by his love which bears the pain of rejection and estrangement, and reaches across the separating abyss which they make. This love-rooted-in-pain compensates for the sundering effects of sin and embraces sinners even at their distance; it exists in an eternal now. The paradoxical blessing of sin is that when we face it and acknowledge it and let it go, it leaves us open to a knowledge of our union. This is part of what Julian of Norwich meant, I think, when she said that our sins would be turned into honours.

Love which is rooted in pain, which in its constancy *will not* reject any part of the beloved, such a love loves all the reality of the sinner's life, can accept all its weaknesses and meanness and cowardice. Trusting to such a love, a sinner can dare to look at his actual life in all its detail and accept that this is what is – because tangible reality is the only possible starting-off place for a new journey. But as soon as he or she does so, the details begin to change, and it becomes a different life. A life of grace, within grace. It becomes an awareness of union.

Throughout the twenty-five years since I discovered this

theology, the words 'the pain of God' have reverberated with meaning for me. I have had to wrestle with Kitamori's Lutheran emphasis upon the experience of God's wrath, and indeed I think that Kitamori did too, for the chapters which are based on his student thesis are markedly harsher than those which end his book. Moreover, he himself reveals the change of view, when he describes Jeremiah as the first man to see the pain of God. For almost all his life, Jeremiah was a prophet of the law. He declared the wrath of God uncompromisingly, and was therefore a 'man of anger', not a 'man of pain'. That surely is how it happens for us. It is the law, the mores of our society, the super-ego, which first governs us. And if we are wounded so that it seems to us that anger was the first thing we received, or so that our own anger is one of the first things we know, then we too are 'men of anger', either as victims or as inflictors. It is only later, with the intimations of forgiving love and our own compunction, that we admit the pain of our estrangement and are guided by it. So too for Jeremiah, who preached God's wrath for forty years, until at last, as chapter 31 of his book reveals, he understood for the first time that God's wrath was completely overcome by his love. 'The word of God which Jeremiah heard at this decisive moment was "my bowels are troubled". God's wrath had passed . . . God's love completely overcame his wrath.'[9] That term from the Authorized Version of the Bible no longer has any real meaning for us; but the New English Bible makes more sense of it by translating it as the heart's yearning: 'As often as I turn my back upon him I still remember him; and so my heart yearns for his, I am filled with tenderness for him.'[10]

How often in this stunning chapter from Jeremiah does God's love and pain break forth (after he has first reminded Israel, in an old formula for old ears, of its sins and his punishment):

> I will cause the new skin to grow and heal your wounds, says the Lord . . . I have dearly loved you from of old, and still I maintain my unfailing care for you . . . They come home, weeping as they come, but I will comfort them and be their escort. I will lead them to flowing

streams; they shall not stumble, their path will be so smooth. For I have become a Father to Israel . . . I will turn their mourning into gladness, I will relent and give them joy to outdo their sorrow.'[11]

Does your own heart yearn when you read this passage? Mine does. With it I am recalled and opened again to my knowledge of the yearning, faithful heart of God; and am so gently admonished on my pilgrim's path: 'Build cairns to mark your way, set up sign-posts; make sure of the road, the path which you will tread . . . How long will you twist and turn, my wayward child? . . . The Lord bless you, the Lord, your true goal, your holy mountain.'[12] Surely God wants us to know that we are loved, forgiven, and encouraged. Kitamori writes about the 'extraordinary proclamation' of the new covenant, which 'plays the most important role not only in *Jeremiah 31* but also in the entire Scripture'. God has expressed his yearning grief for humankind, and he promises overflowing love: 'I will forgive their wrongdoing and remember their sin no more.'[13]

The old covenant, formed in the wrath of God which is the law, was the ethic of obedience. There was no alternative then but to obey the law and avoid the wrath of God, for the people were not aware of the still-hidden 'pain of God' which held them even in their disobedience. But the new covenant, heard by Jeremiah and taught and practised by Jesus, rising out of 'love-rooted-in-the-pain-of-God', is a covenant of creativity, assuring humankind that the disobedience inherent in being human and therefore weak and faltering does not sunder it from that creative love beyond pain, and asking from humankind the response of a creative love in a new ethic.

How long ago Jeremiah spoke to us of the love beyond the law, of the forgiveness which our immature eyes, focused on law and wrath, could not see, and which it seems we still cannot, or will not, see. The message was not just re-told by Jesus; we know that it was fully lived by him. But we seem to find punishment and retribution much more believable. We are still re-finding and re-defining the new covenant.

It is not necessarily that God lacks the power to destroy

us, to punish us, but that in his love for us He has painfully and terribly chosen never to use it. In agony He must stand by and let us be. He intervenes only to help, never to hurt. The Christian God is a God of restraint. Having forsworn the use of power *against* us, if we refuse His help, He has no recourse but, weeping, to watch us punish ourselves.[14]

But *we* do have a recourse – to see his pain and respond to his tears, to want his love, and to repent and change. 'By serving as witness to the pain of God,' Kitamori says, 'our pain is transformed into light; it becomes meaningful and fruitful.'[15] God suffers *with* us because he knows how much we are tried, and he suffers *in* us as sin breaks us. But we can bear witness to the world that God's pain is with us in our separation, and that it is an effective grace. The pain of God 'accepts those who absolutely should not be accepted . . . the pain of God reflects his heart, loving those who should not be loved'[16] because they have turned their backs on him in sin. He loves the sinner who has rejected that love and tried to put himself outside of it, because of its searing gaze upon him, because of his responsibilities to it. 'The pain of God is the tidings that God *still* loves the sinner',[17] no matter what the sinner has done, and is doing. The gospel is the pain of God, Jesus' life was the pain of God, we are the pain of God.

## Responding to the new covenant

God has reached out to us, he is always reaching out to us, and we can reach back in contrite recognition. One way and another, people have always reached back to God in response; but too often they have been taught that they must reach through some intermediary or within some organization. Those who felt that the nature of their response and the actions which it prompted were their own responsibility used to be the rebels or outsiders; now they are the majority, and of this majority, most are probably not church-goers. They are trying to find their own way of commitment. Each generation has to explore its tension between institutional and individual factors in order to find the best way to respond to God's loving invitation, and in our time more and more people want to, or have to, find an individual way. But this need not be an isolated way at all. We learn from each other, and benefit from each other's work. Two thousand years of the churches' doctrines have at least taught us the idea of substitution; whether we agree with it or not, whether we believe it, we are likely to know about it. 'Christ died for our sins.' Somehow, it is said, the death of that man in Jerusalem made a difference to the universe. I believe that it did, and perhaps to a unique degree – but not a unique difference. We are all called to make that sort of difference, to love as he did, to make our actions a daily living substitution, to *expend* our lives for others – even we who probably will not ever be *laying down* our lives for anybody.

We all make a difference, all the time, and our tremendous possibility and responsibility is to make a difference for good. The universe is an intricate and interrelated web of forces beyond our comprehension or even conception, but not beyond our influence. For me, the 'second coming of Christ' will not be the Word again incarnate in a single human body nor even in a single body of glory. But when every person on earth willingly accepts the Spirit into his or her heart and mind and actions, then will the Spirit of Christ at last be fully incarnate. I do not think at all in unique or hierarchical terms, of formal organizations in which specialists are privileged to hold the Body of God, authorized to pass on his forgiveness, committed to intercession. Perhaps they were particularly gifted and skilled in these tasks, perhaps we will not do them as well. Nevertheless, it is time for all of us to do them. Specialization in secular matters is increasingly sensible and productive; but the time has arrived, is indeed long overdue for religious specialization to become less important and for spiritual work to be more and more widely carried out by 'ordinary' people. We are all to become equally responsible for the personal and spiritual well-being of our neighbour, our society, our planet. I think of a sort of spiritual democracy: this bit and that bit are exchanged and substituted, we owe this and that to others, we give this and that into their lives – everybody doing something, no one ever knowing exactly what has been done, either for them or by them; all so very dependent, but never sure upon whom or how effectively. For me, there is not one divine person who did it all, once and forever in time, and one church which can tell us all about it, so that all *we* have to do thereafter is follow and accept. Jesus led the way, showed us that Substitution and Exchange are paths of salvation – and we have to do our own version of what he did.

Compunction was our recognition of just how we had caused our separation from God. For our own sakes, we then had to change what we were doing. That is essential, it is usually the only way to begin; but what it then brings us to is a reason far beyond ourselves for making the efforts of repentance, reconciliation and reparation. Kitamori asks whether the biblical injunctions have seemed like cruel commands: 'Take up your cross and follow me.' 'Serve the pain of God through your own pain.' 'If we fail to understand their real intention, these commands may seem cruel . . . [But their purpose] is to *heal* our pain . . . The Lord has promised that when we bear our cross for him and lose our life for him, we find our life.'[18] It is, of course, our old life that we lose, and a new one which we find, a new life in which we are neither separated nor alone, not from God, our selves, or others. It brings us to a new, and wider, responsibility. Since we are not alone, everything that we do matters to someone, somewhere, for some reason.

In *Original Blessing*, Matthew Fox stresses the importance of 'accepting the truth of ourselves as co-creators with God. This truth recalls on the one hand our immense dignity and on the other our awesome responsibility.'[19] It is as co-creators with God that we have the tremendous responsibility of ensuring that what we bring into the universe, into our society, and into the lives around us, is good. The real harm done by sin is to bring bad instead, to bring falseness, partialness, lack of passion, to lead grey lives. Sin is not often black and dramatic; it is grey. It is the grey life of withholding what one can put into the universe, it is a refusal or a shirking of the requirement to be a co-creator. It is, most tragically, the loss of the joy and value of being a co-creator.

## THE PAIN OF GOD

Charles Williams wrote about the Way of Exchange which was for him the very heart of the Christian religion, which is for me the heart of human life. He taught that we live in one another: co-inherence; that we fulfil our responsibility by living for and by others: the practice of substituted love; and that our joy and wisdom is not to reckon the cost nor to ensure a fair distribution: the way of exchange. None of this is new, of course; but Williams' brilliant exposition of it in a theology of romantic love is profoundly useful in our contemporary setting. Substituted love, he writes, 'might be called "loving from within". One no longer merely loves an object; one has a sense of loving precisely from the great web in which the object and we are both combined.'[20] In a book which draws together Williams' teaching from its many sources, Mary Shideler says, 'Another name for loving from within is compassion – suffering with – which, Williams writes, "is a very great word; it is perhaps the most awful, absolute, and significant of all the names of God in relation to men . . . [and] the most intense name for the unity of men and women".'[21]

'We are continually borne by others. Therefore, willingly or unwillingly we are perpetually in debt to God and to the whole creation.'[22] That is a humbling position to acknowledge; and if we are frightened, demanding, or resentful, it may also be one whose obligations we bitterly resist. The way of exchange is without any normal human limits.

> But the redeemed man has no desire to be free of obligation; gratitude is the taproot of his existence . . . If circumstances provide for his giving where he has received, all is most well. If not, some other will pay his debt and he will pay another's. All is still most well, because the particular joy of mutuality has been replaced by the equal but different joy of extending the pattern of interchange to include others. When one gives to some other person, he may be repaid by a third, perhaps in an entirely different coinage. The precise equity of the kingdom, wherein all is gift, balances the accounts.[23]

This 'unfairness' is very difficult to accept. We want what *we* want, from the person *we* choose to receive from; we want to give to those whom we choose. It is very hard to care about the 'equity of the kingdom' more than about our own desires, but that is what must come as we open and grow outwards. Not 'must' as in yet another imposed standard, but as the inevitable result of the choices for self and God. Perhaps it will be some comfort to you, as it is to me, to reflect that strenuous efforts to be glad are not necessary! Merely do what you can as well as you can, and the glad joy of the kingdom will grow from it.

But it will grow in its own time, which is also difficult to accept, and will come in its own way, not in ours. The way of exchange cannot be predicted. 'Usually the way must be made ready for heaven, and then it will come by some other; the sacrifice must be made ready, and the fire will strike on another altar.'[24] Though we must do all we can to be ready for heaven within ourselves, we cannot know with any certainty when it will come to us, or even perhaps whether it will at all, for we need others or one other to bring to us the fertilizing idea, the loving experience, the shock of growth. All we can do is the work to hand, and perhaps what we will eventually find is that our work was preparing us for the unexpected heaven which someone else is to bring to us; or we can purge and discipline ourselves, we can face what we have to do or to give up, and still our transformation may not occur – but someone else, benefiting from our example or our effort, blazes into fulfilment. It is a dreadfully hard lesson, learning to do without the benefits which we wanted from our own struggle, or to be glad of the joy which someone brings to us even when it is not the one we looked for, or to be satisfied that our effort has brought good, even though not, this time, to ourselves.

It is awesome to discover how, on the way of exchange, one can be relieved of a burden of pain by someone who says only, 'Let go of it for a while; I'm here'; or how sometimes one carries – rather than suffers – the consequences of another's actions. Perhaps we should not ever try to carry the sin of someone who *will not* attempt to surrender it to God, nor ask anyone to give us that sort of support, because only the refuser can or should undo a willed refusal; but Shideler describes what Williams means by the bearing of another's sin for a while at least, when he *cannot* undo it himself:

> The bearer makes of himself a way by which the sin can be taken into God: he assumes to himself the responsibility and the consequences of the sin, not in the pretence that he had committed it, and not because he is his brother's keeper or even because he is his brother's brother, but because he partakes of his brother's life. They co-inhere, each in the other, so that one can do what the other – for whatever reason – cannot, and so he does it.[25]

The process is mysterious, but not inexplicable: 'The sin is not wiped out, but its energy is re-directed. Sinful man is not destroyed but changed – and changed by the introduction of another energy that counteracts the energy of . . . sin.'[26]

It is the same, too, in the bearing of one another's burdens, as St Paul said was the law of Christ,[27] or – rare and difficult and strange – allowing another to carry ours. Even when there is no material action involved, this is a very real exchange, a precise spiritual equivalent of any friendly task. We hand over a burden of fear, pain, guilt or anxiety just as we would ask and trust another to do any task for us: 'Essentially there is no difference between asking a friend to carry one's fear, and hiring someone to scrub a floor, or ordering a subordinate to draft a report, or letting a neighbour run an errand. All these are forms of substitution: A substitutes his labour for B's. If there is love on the part of either, this is substituted love.'[28] What an enormous trust this involves! After the initial honesty about what the burden is, which is in itself difficult, one then trusts the other to carry it truly, and most of all, trusts the situation enough to be without the burden and to discover what will happen to oneself without it. Imagine, for example, trusting someone else to carry your guilt. Imagine, when he or she has done so, saying to yourself, 'I don't have any guilt now' – and then having to do what is right and appropriate to the guilt-free state. You might well find out why you had been harbouring the guilt, before this revealing experiment! Bearing another's burdens is so familiar an idea as to have lost its aweful implications; but approaching it from the angle of letting go of our own is revealing.

But bearing one another's burdens is just one part of substitution. There is also carrying another's joy during a period when he cannot remember or feel it; there is carrying another's shame or penitence when he or she cannot confess it. In exchange, there is the willingness to surrender our own achievement or harvest if our work has brought it to another instead; letting another do what we wanted to do ourselves because he or she can do it better, is in a more suitable place to do it, has been asked by others to do it. The way of exchange is central to the Christian belief in one who endured agony for those he loved beyond all limits and who brought them freedom and joy. It is central to a belief in a creative and merciful God who upholds all the movements of life and draws them towards fulfilment; and central also to the humanitarian principles which give birth to so much of the good will and good effort to relieve the world's suffering from social evil and natural disaster.

### Pain and the breadth of exchange

When God blessed Noah and his sons, he also laid an obligation upon them: 'At the hand of every man's brother will I require the life of man.'[29] Understood for millennia as the exchange of a death for a death, this command is horrifying, and so is the God who commanded it explicitly as the shedding of blood. Or so – I would prefer to think – is the understanding which heard and recorded it thus. But as I hear it, every man is responsible for the life of his brother, for the livingness of his brother, or sister, his friend, or neighbour, or enemy. This early declaration of exchange is that of an *exchange of responsibility*. Every person is responsible to some extent, and sometimes to a very great extent, for the degree and quality of the livingness of others. 'It is impossible for one person to sin and others to remain unaffected. There is not only a psychosomatic unity within each individual, but a unity of human beings, and

even more widely, a unity with all of creation.' The
fracture which is the result of sin is not just personal
on into society and onto the planet and throughout t

But it is equally true that the healing of that fract
far beyond the personal. When we have seen and understood
and tried to undo the harm which we had caused to livingness,
the time comes for our positive contribution of goodness and
creativity. When we have been broken open by compunction
and have felt the new life of grace, we can let go of our narrow
egocentrism, especially in any preoccupation with our past sin
or an excessive preoccupation with its remaining elements. We
can hand that burden on to God, through Christ if he is our
mediator, or in simple personal surrender of it, if that is our
way. Now we can look outside and beyond ourselves. There
comes a time for us to work deliberately and consciously for a
new perspective and for the growth of our vision, because we
have learned what the darkness had to teach and the time has
come to let it go, if it will. Our eyes can be set upon the vision
which each of us brings out of our struggles, and we can move
now with a right energy into wider understanding, ability and
contribution. We can travel all the way out of the darkness,
planting apple trees as we go, making a legacy of livingness in
relationship with all of creation, which is the co-inherence.

> Blessing involves relationship: one does not bless without
> investing something of oneself into the receiver of one's
> blessing. And one does not receive blessing oblivious of
> its gracious giver. A blessing spirituality is a relating spiri-
> tuality. And if it is true that all of creation flows from a
> single, loving source, then all of creation is blessed and is
> a blessing, atom to atom, molecule to molecule, organism
> to organism, land to plants, plants to animals, animals
> to other animals, people to people, and back to atoms,
> molecules, plants, fishes.[31]

After the estrangement and harm of sin, forgiveness is the
primary exchange, the realization of enduring relationship or
the restoration of a broken one and the shared gladness of
reconciliation. It is a primary blessing, of great sweetness and

recognition; it affirms us, and the value of what has happened to us, the value even of our darkness and pain. We need not regret our pain, not even the pain of sin, nor fear that it was a waste, nor believe that we could have learned better in some other way. Those who have begun to understand the pain of God, because they have explored and integrated their own pain in their growth out of sin, can witness to the 'ethic of pain' as a part of the 'ethic of creativity', and of the creative, responsible life entirely. Fox appreciates an image from a Japanese poet who says that 'we must embrace pain and burn it as a fuel for our journey'.[32]

> Unwished-for pain, provided we pray it or enter into it and do not cover it up and run from it, can often bring that love of life back to us . . . There is a strength learned from suffering that cannot be learned in any other way. For suffering tests the depth of our love of life and relationship even when and especially because relationships are so often the cause of our suffering . . . The purpose of letting pain be pain is precisely this: to let go of pain . . . Ideally, by entering into it we become able to breathe so much freedom from within the pain that the deepest kind of letting go can truly occur. For this to happen, the naming of the pain, the letting it be pain for a while, is essential.[33]

In his own wrestling with the horror and meaning of sin, Kazoh Kitamori recognizes that it is difficult to heal our pain when we cannot find comparisons or metaphors to describe it. But indeed we need something more than that; we need a symbol, that is, an image, thought, or action through which we take part in divine processes, what Jung called 'the best and highest possible expression of something divined but not yet known even to the observer'.[34] 'A symbol witnesses to divine truth by uniting human and divine truth', says Kitamori.[35] The pain of God is just such a symbol, and is all the more effective because it so explicitly includes us as part of the relationship. 'Man's pain becomes a symbol of the pain of God because God and man are united through the condition of pain . . . this union takes place in *estrangement*.'[36] More precisely, the pain of *our* estrangement reveals *God's* unbroken union with us. Our early pain about sin is the pain of separation; it is, typically, egotistical, and its helpfulness is therefore limited. But when we start to look at the pain of God, we simply cannot remain so small-minded! A whole universe of love opens up for us when we share God's pain with him, because we gaze clear-sightedly at our sin and its consequences, and long to lessen the pain which we cause to God, to our true selves, and to others. When it is no longer only *our* pain of separation which we want to overcome, but also *their* pain of holding us and waiting for us, the whole colour and emphasis of our lives is changed.

There is a sense in which we could say that our sin, which had been disguised, denied, and rationalized, is transformed into *redemptive sin* by compunction. That is the time when we strongly feel the estrangement and recognize in it the 'wrath of God' – that is, the inevitable effects of sin in us – *and when we respond with love and not with fear and resentment*, thus giving to ourselves the symbol which will unite us with God's love-rooted-in-pain. When we feel compunction and respond to forgiveness, we become living symbols of something we only sense but cannot define, and our lives have an influence for good beyond their objectively observed effects, just as in sin their influence was pervasive but only partly observable.

Remember that Teilhard de Chardin warned us that 'there is no end to the tearing up of roots that is involved on our journey'.[37] If you take seriously the attitudes and interpretations which we have been discussing in this book, you will find that it will not be just a matter of tearing out the present sins, so that life is thereafter cleaner, straighter, and easier. A *process* of tearing up of roots will have begun, and there is no predicting the end of that. 'We must think deeply', says Kitamori, 'about the result of being captured in "the pain of God" – the love of God who accepts his own sinners who are turning their backs on him.'[38] What a splendid idea! We are captured by God's love-rooted-in-pain, we cannot escape however we try and however we seem to have succeeded. It is not that a hound of heaven pursues us and will eventually catch us, but that we have nowhere to run because the whole universe is a corral of love. We are completely enclosed by it.

Because God's reaching out to us is *love*-rooted-in-pain it is filled with light, welcoming and enabling. Oh, we feel the pain of it, right enough, but we all know that there is inescapably a great deal of pain in life – our choice is whether it is to be a grey, miserable, self-diminishing pain or a sharp and cleansing pain that opens us and helps us to become filled with our true selves.

In a sense we intercede for ourselves when we bear the pain of our sin and our painful knowledge of its consequences, and reach from our side across to God in a 'love-which-is-rooted-in-pain'. Our true self, which knows goodness and our own goodness, reaches out to God to intercede for the weak and wrongdoing part of ourselves, and helps it to accept its pain as a symbol for God's pain, a recognition of estranged love.

Our pain and our compunction, our repentance and reparation, are a process of giving birth to God in our own lives. The person burdened or darkened by sin does not bear God within himself or herself, does not bear God as presence, God as loved one, God as the one to work for and with. But the pilgrim or explorer gives birth to God in his or her spirit in the struggle against, and the surrender of, sin. He or she makes a place for God to inhabit, opens it for God to enter, keeps it ready for God to grow in, and acts from it so that God is born into the world. This is one of the deepest reasons for struggling against sin: so that we become able to take part in God's coming to birth in the world, through our willing spirits, into the family we belong to, into our community, into the wider society and the family of nations.

### 'Thy kingdom come'

One of the most important prefixes in the language is 'inter-'. Interdependence, interaction, interpenetration, intermingle – we would be mistaken to look at any part of the world and see it in isolation. Every part is always acting and being acted upon, in simultaneous relationship with numerous other parts; every one helping to create others through sustenance, influence, attrition, deprivation. It is a ceaseless and total creation.

This is why I respond to the concept of interchange in Charles Williams' work. I would never advocate a selfless 'life of giving'; completely self-abnegating generosity is a vocation for very few. That is not to diminish the necessity and value of giving. To give to others without return is undoubtedly an important discipline and an aspect of all spiritual growth, and when it is directed towards those who cannot offer a return (or at least not an equivalent one), such as children or the very aged or the many recipients of charity, then it is quite simply necessary to human life. But a concentration upon giving would make for a very narrow way of life! It is as blessed and as necessary to receive lovingly as it is to give; it is as liberating to ask for what one needs or wants as it is to offer before being asked; it is humanly enlarging both to receive with gladness and to pass on willingly the best of what one has received. The true growth of the kingdom of God on earth depends not upon giving but upon the life of exchange. When every person gives all that he or she can, not to make the bookkeeping balance but out of overflowing generosity and glad receiving, and every person has both hands busy – one hand giving and the other joyously accepting – then the energy of Love is able to flow freely in the universe and to enrich all of humankind.

Our responsibility is to ensure that what is exchanged is good and life-enhancing, that we do not hand on harmfulness but through our creative suffering remove its poison from the web of interchange.

> Sin, one learns from reflection on the Via Positiva, would consist in injuring creation and doing harm to its balance and harmoniousness, turning what is beautiful into what is ugly. In this sense all ecological damage is a sin against the Via Positiva and . . . such a sin is a break, a rupture, in creation itself. It represents the most basic injustice, that of humanity to its own source, the earth . . . The sinful consciousness that lies behind ecological sin is that of a

dualistic mentality that treats other creatures in a subject/object fashion of manipulation and control.[39]

Interchange is entirely different from the dualist mentality, the estrangement of me-here and you-there. It is an infinite network where every part depends upon and sustains the other parts, where damage expands like shock waves unless it is limited by sacrifice, and goodness reverberates from part to part in a carillon of creativity. 'Beauty has to do with seeing all life as blessing, with returning blessing for blessing, with forging blessing of pain and suffering and tragedy and loss. Beauty needs to be made and remade. It is the vital work of the artist within ourselves.'[40]

Teilhard de Chardin wrote of 'the birth of a new spiritual reality formed by souls *and the matter they draw after them*'.[41] We are not a duality of soul and body, but a complementarity in which soul forms matter and matter expresses soul, and the whole is the body of God. Each person we relate to for good or ill is changed by us in his material life and his spirit; every material thing we touch is changed to some extent, and how can we know how much spirit is changed with it? In eternity, which is timelessness, spacelessness, the unlimited habitation of the Limitless, everything which can ever be, already is; but it is we who determine what will become manifest from it. We are each a minute but unique and precious fragment of that heavenly fulfilment on earth. It is not possible wholly to escape the painful disjunction between the timeless events of heaven and their distorted or inadequate happening on earth, within time. To be aware of that disjunction is to suffer the effects of sin – that is, of the refusal of earthly events and the people in them to bring time into alignment with eternity. But to remain aware of it, in prayer and love and the efforts of living, is to share in the pain of God. Our individual experiences of our own sin make us capable of perceiving the disjunction, and give us the chance to lessen it. The kingdom will have come on earth when that disjointed double image fuses into one.

All goodness expressed in actions hastens the kingdom of God, just as all evil works lengthen humankind's separation from him. We cannot see, now, how much of our work and pain are contributing to this mystic end; but out of the brokenness and sin which seemed so dark and unpromising when we started this exploration there grows a way in which the spirit of God within us can return to God, uniting humankind and the divine.

> Wholly given to Love, at least trying at each moment to choose the death that leads to life instead of the pseudo-life that leads to death, you are filled with the power of the spirit: you know, or begin to know, in yourself the freedom of the sons of God; you become, or begin to become, in truth an . . . apt instrument for the spirit's life-giving work . . .
>
> Slowly, constantly thwarted by our perversity and blindness and evil but still continuing, the revelation of love's meaning goes on. Evil produces its ineluctable consequences, and the world is drenched with pain; but at every point in time and space where pain has its kingdom, there also are the tears of God, and sooner or later through the tears the soul of the world is renewed.[42]

# EPILOGUE: TRAVELLER'S HARVEST

'Herein is that saying true, one soweth and another reapeth. I sent you to reap that whereon ye bestowed no labour; other men laboured and ye are entered into their labours.' What! after self-sacrifice and crosses and giving up goods and life, the mind perplexed, the heart broken, the body wrecked – is there not a little success of our own, our own in him, of course, but at least his in us? None: 'I sent you to reap whereon ye bestowed no labour.' The harvest is of others, as the beginning was in others, and the process was by others. This man's patience shall adorn that man, and that man's celerity this; and magnificence and thrift exchanged; and chastity and generosity; and tenderness and truth, and so on through the kingdom. We shall be graced by one and by all, only never by ourselves . . . [1]

I have always been felled by that passage from Charles Williams about the way of exchange; its words hammer on my heart. On the surface it seems to say that all the *good* we have will come through the work of others: both those who sow and those who reap will *rejoice* in the harvest. But there is a sombre other side to the image: if what one person sows is the whirlwind, *that* is what another will reap, and if one sows joy, it is *another* who may feed off it. We are all dependent on what others have sown, and we cannot be sure of the harvest even of our own good husbandry. For Williams, life is all substitution and exchange, and we have very little say in what we are to receive or can retain. That is an outlook of such bleak helplessness – from the view of each needy, struggling individual – that at times I can hardly bear it. Yet I have returned again and again to this passage for its truth and strength and, strangely, I return when I feel most un-nourished. I realize now that I do so because in this, as in all of Williams' teaching, I receive a gift which proves much deeper and more enduring than what, in my too narrow perspective, had seemed to be my needs. The greater need in trouble and pain is always for a more than personal viewpoint. It is for a vision of meaning and purpose. Job lost health and family and property, but his greatest suffering was the meaninglessness of his suffering.

Williams tells us that somehow our pain and loss, our torture from guilt, our effort to overcome sin, are valuable because there *is* a harvest, there always is. It may well not be ours, and we may never even see it, because there is no knowing where and how it will flourish. 'The vicarious life of the Kingdom is not necessarily confined to sequence even among the human members of the Kingdom. The past and the future are subject to interchange, as the present with both, the dead with the living, the living with the dead . . . '[2] But in the very attempt to understand and to care about the harvest more than our pre-specified share of it, we become open and receptive in a new way, and discover an unexpected fruitfulness. And *then* we find that a new willingness is asked of us: to let go of whatever it is we have wanted and to welcome whatever grace has brought from the unseen labour of others to answer our own labours. 'There is no such thing as "my" bread. All bread is *ours* and is given to me, to others through me and to me through others. For not only bread but all things necessary for sustenance in this life are given on loan to us with others, and because of others and for others and to others through us.'[3]

Oh, truly I do know that this is not an easy thing to learn; it is an almost daily effort, for a long time. And have we come to an end of the struggle with sin only to be faced with another? Well—yes. The work of life towards, for, and with God does not end. It is just that we are given new tasks fitted to our greater responsibility, made to face newly-seen weaknesses from which we will wrest more reliable abilities, discover new countries of experience where the light is clearer and the path surer.

> Work is always accompanied by the painful pangs of birth . . . To create, or organise, material energy, or truth, or beauty, brings with it an inner torment which prevents those who face its hazards from sinking into the quiet and closed-in life wherein grows the vice of self-regard . . . An honest workman not only surrenders his calm and peace once and for all, but must learn continually to jettison the form which his labour or art first took, and go in search of new forms . . . Over and over again he must go beyond himself, tear himself away from himself, leaving behind him his most cherished beginnings . . .
>
> The more nobly a man wills and acts, the more avid he becomes for great and sublime aims to pursue . . . He will want wider organisations to create, new paths to blaze, causes to uphold, truths to discover, an ideal to cherish and defend. So, gradually, the worker no longer belongs to himself. Little by little the great breadth of the universe has insinuated itself into him through the fissure of his humble but faithful action, has broadened him, raised him up, borne him on.[4]

A few years ago, when I felt a strong obligation to stand by someone who was doing most dreadful wrong, and not least to himself, I had a picture of myself as, perhaps, a wartime resistance worker with orders from unknown leaders, waiting at a remote border crossing:

> I have called and called into the darkness,
> and no one came.
> I brought a passport, as I was told to do,
> and waited beyond the hour;
> I brought food and clothing and greetings
> – they had told me to wait.
> But nothing has moved in the darkness.

## EPILOGUE

>Oh, masters, I am weary.
>What good can I do here?
>I haven't delivered your message,
>or reached into the dark –
>what good can I do here?
>
>I am a herald without reverberation.

I still do not know if I did any good, or at least enough to make some difference; it is very possible that I never will know. If I did, it is even more possible that another will reap the harvest with my friend, wherever he is. But I stayed, then, because more than twenty years before this experience, someone else had stayed by me in my own wrongdoing, and had changed my life forever by that faithfulness to the truth. I hope that I may have made a change in this life for which I felt a responsibility. I hope that I was taking part, at the desolate border crossing, in an exchange which may be fruitful even during mortal, personal life: certainly I believe that it was and remains truly an exchange in the life of God's mysterious, loving universe of relationship. That belief is what that effort brought to me.

Mine is a sombre vision, not so much by nature as by experience. It has seemed to me that my family sowed bitterness and wounding, and that my job has been to reap it and to let fall as little of it as I could manage, so that it should not sprout again in the next year's crop. I have ploughed, sown, and weeded a score of derelict fields, and when I am discouraged it seems that I do not reap any good harvest from that work, nor even (when I am lonely) that I have the gratification of seeing another do so. Yet look at me in this hour: I sit here writing out of my experience to you whom I shall never see, and the love passes from a friend of thirty years ago to you for something perhaps in your next thirty years. Though it is not the one I expected from those fields, is this not a harvest indeed? Too often we name ahead of time the outcome we want, from each struggle on our journey, and when it turns out to be a different one we do not recognize the blessing in it. Because the blessing is not in the particular harvest, but in the exchange itself.

I stayed in that equivocal situation because there was some small hope that, unseen, my patience might become my friend's strength. Why should it have mattered so? I cannot argue for the why: I can only state the belief – that we are called to the way of exchange, and neither the call nor our service are dependent upon our understanding what is exchanged, nor even whether it has truly passed from us to another. We are to be there, we are to try. That is our contribution to the heartbeat of a universe of love, and of pain.

A damaged child grows into a perception of his parents' motives which they will never acknowledge, and his understanding takes up some of their responsibility. A woman tends her senile mother, drawing from memories of a loving grandmother enough forgiveness to accept the unfair accusations of old age. A deserted lover goes to a counsellor for help in examining his own part in the failure. Good-hearted and ashamed neighbours try clumsily to compensate a black family for attacks in the school playground. Social workers pick up the pieces after society's neglect and wear themselves out in thankless patching-up. A student goes into the firing line of what has become a riot in the hope of at least learning the names of the dead. A contemplative nun puts her soul into some torn place in the spiritual world, to carry an unknown sufferer's pain. They are all exchanging, and grace is in every act, prompting, sustaining, and fulfilling the human aspiration.

> By his fidelity he must *build* – starting with the most natural territory of his own self – a work, an *opus*, into which something enters from all the elements of the earth. *He makes his own soul* throughout all his earthly days; and at the same time he collaborates in another work, another *opus*, which infinitely transcends, while at the same time it narrowly determines, the perspectives of his individual achievement: the completing of the world.[5]

Early in this book I questioned the 'ethic of obedience'. We must examine, I said, what it is we obey, and decide for ourselves whether it deserves that commitment from us. But the outcome of our examination might well be the need to make our own road in creative exploration, risking error and failure, working always to make something new and valuable out of our uncertainty. 'Beauty is born out of the coupling of love of life and its harmonies with pain at life and its discords.'[6] Out of that creative effort of love and pain, I have found, one reaches a new obedience: sensitive, responsive, eager to see clearly, humbly aware of dependence and vulnerability. It is the obedience of the self saying 'Yes' to the spirit of Love, and Truth, and Reality. It is not caused by any fearful guilt of mine, nor a giving in to the unpredictable power of another, nor fear of exclusion from a community unless I conform. Instead, what holds me to it is an aching sorrow in the very heart of my soul whenever I stray from its central grace.

This is my last page. We have come to the end of that part of the journey which we can make together. I do not know where it will take us now; but if you have been changed, however slightly, in the reading of this book as I have been by the writing of it, then some part of us will be together during the rest of our travelling on the path of Blessing Exchanged.

# FURTHER READING

The model of psychological development which I present here is based upon the work of a group of British psychoanalysts and psychotherapists of the 'object-relations' school: Fairbairn, Winnicott, Guntrip, and especially Frank Lake. Readers who have found this model helpful might be interested in the following reading list, which includes these writers, and others who have, for me, expanded the understanding which I obtained from that basic structure.

## General psychological understanding for lay people:

**Bryant, Christopher**, *The Heart in Pilgrimage: Christian Guidelines for the Human Journey* (London, Darton, Longman & Todd, 1980)
A deeply wise and heartening book by a member of the Society of St John the Evangelist (the Cowley Fathers). *The River Within* can also be recommended.
**Frankl, Viktor**, *The Doctor and the Soul: From Psychotherapy to Logotherapy* (New York, Vintage Books, 1973)
'A new approach to the neurotic personality which emphasizes man's spiritual values and the quest for meaning in life.'
— *The Unconscious God* (London, Hodder & Stoughton, 1975)
'The founder of logotherapy and world-famous psychiatrist explores the reality and significance to all men of the concept of God.'
— *The Will to Meaning* (New York, Plume/New American Library, 1969)
A very useful way to consider the psycho-spiritual nature of human beings. Although Frankl is a psychiatrist, I have included him in this list because I do not think that these books are particularly technical.
**Hardy, Jean**, *A Psychology with a Soul* (London, Routledge & Kegan Paul, 1987)
Roberto Assagioli also worked at the interface between psychology and spirituality, but wrote little himself. Hardy's book is a fine overview of his thought.

**Jones, Alan**, *Soul Making: The Desert Way of Spirituality* (London, SCM Press, 1985)
An absolutely splendid and inspiring book to which I am much indebted.
**Martin, P. W.**, *Experiment in Depth: A Study of the Work of Jung, Eliot and Toynbee* (London, Routledge & Kegan Paul, 1976)
Object-relations psychology looks back at how we got to where we are; Jung, essentially, looks at where we are and ahead to where we can go. This is a demanding but valuable examination of religion and Jung's depth psychology.
**Singer, June**, *Boundaries of the Soul: The Practice of Jung's Psychology* (New York, Anchor Books, 1973)
This is the best introduction I have found to Jung's work, and is a useful view of the spiritual life from the psychological angle.
**Tillich, Paul**, *The Courage to Be* (London, Fontana, 1962)
This classic of modern theology is remarkably helpful to anyone trying to understand themselves both psychologically and spiritually.

## Technical psychoanalytical books:

**Fairbairn, W. Ronald D.**, *An Object-Relations Theory of the Personality* (New York, Basic Books, 1954)
—*Psychoanalytical Studies of the Personality* (London, Tavistock Publications, 1952)
Pioneering work.
**Guntrip, Harry J. S.**, *Psychoanalytic Theory, Therapy and the Self* (London, Hogarth Press, 1971)
—*Personality Structure and Human Interaction* (London, Hogarth Press, 1961)
My catalogue card for this book states simply, 'Stupendous!' The last chapters are especially useful for their examination of how the infant psyche can choose to hide completely from pain.
—*Schizoid Phenomena, Object Relations and the Self* (London, Hogarth Press, 1968)
A most profound study of desolation and dereliction. Guntrip's origins as a minister are evident in his great compassion. His *Psychology for Ministers and Social Workers* (George Allen & Unwin 1971) is a useful introduction to his work.
**Lake, Frank**, *Clinical Theology: A Theological and Psychological Basis to Clinical Pastoral Care* (London, Darton, Longman & Todd, 1966)
This is the book which for me put the keystone in the arch. A massive study of personal development and its major distresses, from a Christian viewpoint; the chapters which examine the Dark Night of the Spirit in the light of schizoid dereliction and isolation are invaluable – but are cut by three-quarters in the abridged edition (Darton, Longman & Todd,

1986). The latter is better than nothing; but try to get the former through your Public Library Interloan service.

**Winnicott, D. W.**, *Collected Papers: Through Paediatrics to Psychoanalysis* (London, Tavistock, 1958)

— *The Maturational Processes and the Facilitating Environment: Studies in the Theory of Emotional Development* (London, Hogarth Press, 1965)

Carried forward Fairbairn's work. Some of the papers are very interesting indeed.

# NOTES

The first time that a book is cited, the reference will be asterisked, and will include the bibliographical information, which will be omitted thereafter.

**Prologue: Pilgrims and Explorers**

1. I would be grateful to anyone who could tell me the source of this beautiful sentence, jotted down on a scrap of paper years ago.
2. Hebrews 11:13, Authorized Version.

**1: Sin and Guilt — and Choice**

1. *Gerard Hughes, *God of Surprises* (Darton, Longman & Todd 1985), pp. 66–7.
2. 1 John 3:4, New English Bible.
3. Gerard Hughes, *God of Surprises*.
4. Ninth Article, the Thirty-nine Articles of the Church of England.
5. *Stephen T. Davis (ed), *Encountering Evil* (T. & T. Clark 1981), p. 86.
6. *Erich Fromm, *The Heart of Man: Its Genius for Good and Evil* (Routledge & Kegan Paul 1965), p. 123.
7. George Fox, 1656. From *Christian faith & practice in the experience of the Society of Friends* (London Yearly Meeting 1960), Extract 376.
8. *Christopher Bryant, *The Heart in Pilgrimage: Christian Guidelines for the Human Journey* (Darton, Longman & Todd 1980).
9. *Mary McDermott Shideler, *The Theology of Romantic Love: a study in the writings of Charles Williams* (Grand Rapids, Michigan, William B. Eerdmans Publishing Company, 1962), p. 113.
10. *Stephen Hobhouse (ed), *Selected Writings of William Law*, Letter IV, quoted by Charles Williams in *The Forgiveness of Sins*, p. 152.
11. Revd Joy Croft, of the Unitarian Church Centre, Glasgow.

NOTES

12. I am indebted to ★M. Scott Peck, in *People of the Lie: The hope for healing human evil* (Rider 1983), for the phrase which finally clarified my definition: 'Since he refused to acknowledge his imperfection, it was inevitable that Cain, like Satan, should take the law into his own hands and commit murder. In some similar, though usually more subtle fashion, all who are evil also take the law into their own hands, to destroy life or liveliness in defense [sic] of their narcissistic self-image.' (p. 79)
13. ★Simone Weil, *Gravity and Grace* (Routledge & Kegan Paul 1952), p. 69.
14. Jean Clark, psychotherapist.
15. Erich Fromm, *The Heart of Man*, p. 138.
16. ★Harry Guntrip, *Schizoid Phenomena, Object Relations and the Self* (Hogarth Press 1980), p. 142.
17. M. Scott Peck, *People of the Lie*, p. 72.
18. Harry Guntrip, *Schizoid Phenomena*, p. 142.
19. Anyone wanting to follow up the subject of unjustified guilt could try the following: Most of Alice Miller's work on abused children; ★Pierre Solignac (translated by John Bowden), *The Christian Neurosis* (SCM Press 1982); ★J. Conrad Stettbacher, *Making Sense of Suffering* (Dutton 1991); ★Brian Thorne, chapters 7 & 8 of *Person-Centred Counselling: Therapeutic and Spiritual Dimensions* (Whurr Publishers 1991); ★Paul Tournier, *Guilt and Grace* (Hodder & Stoughton 1962).
20. ★Edmund Colledge and James Walsh (eds), *Julian of Norwich. Showings* (Paulist Press 1978), p. 187, Seventh Chapter (Long text).
21. M. Scott Peck, *People of the Lie*, p. 69.
22. ibid. p. 70.
23. ibid. p. 71.
24. ★James Hillman, *Insearch: Psychology and Religion* (Hodder & Stoughton 1967).
25. Christopher Bryant, *The Heart in Pilgrimage*, p. 47.
26. M. Scott Peck, *People of the Lie*, p. 72 & p. 76.
27. Mary Shideler, *The Theology of Romantic Love*, p. 113.
28. M. Scott Peck, *People of the Lie*, p. 67.
29. Erich Fromm, *The Heart of Man*, p. 19.
30. ★Teilhard de Chardin, *Human Energy* (Harcourt Brace Janovitch 1969) (my italics).
31. ★Georges Bernanos, *Diary of a Country Priest* (The Religious Book Club 1937), p. 179.
32. ★Alan Jones, *Soul Making: The Desert Way of Spirituality* (SCM Press 1985), p. 155.

# NOTES

## 2: Two Ethics

1. *Paul Tillich, *Morality and Beyond* (Routledge & Kegan Paul 1964), p. 27.
2. *John Sanford, *The Man Who Wrestled with God: Light from the Old Testament on the Psychology of Religion* (Paulist Press 1987), p. 17.
3. *Harold S. Kushner, *When Bad Things Happen to Good People* (Pan Books Ltd 1981), p. 86.
4. Paul Tillich, *Morality and Beyond*, p. 93.
5. *Paul Tillich, *The Boundaries of Our Being* (Fontana 1973), p. 127.
6. *Carl Gustav Jung, 'The Relations between the Ego and the Unconscious' in *Two Essays on Analytical Psychology* (Routledge & Kegan Paul 1953), p. 237.
7. *William H. Sheldon, *Psychology and the Promethean Will: A Constructive Study of the Acute Common Problem of Education, Medicine and Religion* (Harper & Brothers 1936), p. 5.
8. Margaret Fell, from *Christian faith and practice*, Excerpt 20 (my italics).
9. John Sanford, *The Man Who Wrestled with God*, p. 17.
10. *Dag Hammarskjöld, *Markings* (Faber & Faber 1964), p. 158.
11. Paul Tillich, *Morality and Beyond*, p. 81 (my italics).
12. ibid. p. 23.
13. An Orthodox priest quoted in *John Lampen, *Waiting in the Light* (Quaker Home Service 1981), p. 40.
14. *William Eckhardt, *Compassion: Towards a Science of Value* (Oakville, Ontario, Canadian Peace Research Institute, 1972), p. 255.
15. Epistle from a meeting of elders at Balby to 'the brethren of the north', 1656, from *Christian faith and practice*.

## 3: The Womb of the Spirit

1. Paraphrasing of Romans 7:15.
2. *Frank Lake, *Clinical Theology: A Theological and Psychiatric Basis to Clinical and Pastoral Care* (Darton, Longman & Todd 1966), from the chart 'The dynamics of the nursing couple'.
3. ibid. chart.
4. *Oliver Sacks, *Awakenings* (Duckworth 1973), preface to the original edition.
5. William Eckhardt, *Compassion*, p. 91.
6. Frank Lake, *Clinical Theology*.
7. ibid. p. 177.
8. Harry Guntrip, *Schizoid Phenomena*, pp. 149–50.
9. *Valerie Saiving, 'The Human Situation: A Feminine View' in Carol P. Christ and Judith Plaistow (eds), *Womanspirit Rising: A Feminist Reader in Religion* (New York, Harper, 1992), p. 37.

## NOTES

10. Frank Lake, *Clinical Theology*, p. 1102.
11. ibid. p. 147.
12. ibid. p. 133.
13. *Alice Miller, *Banished Knowledge: Facing Childhood Injuries* (Virago Press 1991), p. 74.
14. William Eckhardt, *Compassion*, p. 86.
15. Frank Lake, *Clinical Theology*, p. 175.
16. Alice Miller, *Banished Knowledge*, p. 51.


## 4: Masks, Knots and Bruises

1. Frank Lake, *Clinical Theology*, p. 162.
2. ibid. p. 162.
3. ibid. p. 156.
4. ibid. p. 158.
5. *Harry Guntrip, *Mental Pain and the Cure of Souls* (London, Independent Press Ltd, 1956), p. 64.
6. ibid. p. 64.
7. Alan Jones, *Soul Making*, p. 34.
8. ibid. p. 35.
9. Georges Bernanos, *Diary of a Country Priest*, p. 120.
10. Galatians 5:22–23, New International Version.
11. *Brian Thorne, *Behold the Man: A therapist's meditations on the Passion of Jesus Christ* (Darton, Longman & Todd 1991), p. 22.
12. Alan Jones, *Soul Making*, p. 35.
13. ibid. p. 87.
14. *Harry Williams, *Some Day I'll Find You* (Mitchell Beazley 1982).
15. Brother Jacint, Communitat del Mas Blanc, Catalunya.
16. Frank Lake, *Clinical Theology*, p. xxvii.


## 5: Paradoxical Wounds

1. Alan Jones, *Soul Making*, p. 43.
2. *Matthew Fox, *Original Blessing: A Primer in Creation Spirituality* (Bear & Company 1983), p. 260. UK edition published in conjunction with Mountain Books, London and available from Element Books, Shaftesbury.
3. ibid. p. 261.
4. ibid. p. 262.
5. *Elie Weisel, *Four Hasidic Masters and Their Struggle Against Melancholy* (Notre Dame, University of Notre Dame Press, 1978), p. 60.
6. Frank Lake, *Clinical Theology*, p. 733.

## NOTES

7. *Søren Kierkegaard, *The Concept of Dread* (Princeton University Press 1946), p. 142.
8. Frank Lake, *Clinical Theology*, p. 734 & p. 759.
9. Matthew Fox, *Original Blessing*, p. 110.
10. Colledge & Walsh, *Julian of Norwich. Showings*, p. 154, Chapter xvii (Short text).
11. *M. Scott Peck, *The Road Less Travelled* (Rider & Co 1978), p. 278.
12. *Alan Wilkinson, 'Christianity and Psychotherapy' in *New Fire*, Vol iii, No 25 (Winter 1975).

### 6: A Blow to the Heart

1. Alan Jones, *Soul Making*, p. 83.
2. *Jacob Needleman, *Lost Christianity* (Bantam New Age Books 1982), p. 170, quoted in Alan Jones, *Soul Making*, p. 89.
3. Alan Jones, *Soul Making*, p. 94.
4. Erich Fromm, *The Heart of Man*, p. 132.
5. Colledge & Walsh, *Julian of Norwich. Showings*, p. 267, Fifty-first Chapter (Long text).
6. *Grace Jantzen, *Julian of Norwich: Mystic and Theologian* (SPCK 1987), p. 194.
7. Revelation 3:20, Authorized Version.
8. *Timothy Ware, *The Orthodox Church* (Penguin Books 1963, reprinted 1987), p. 227.
9. *Morton Kelsey, *The Other Side of Silence: A Guide to Christian Meditation* (New York, Paulist Press, 1976), p. 58.
10. ibid. p. 58.
11. Gerard Hughes, *God of Surprises*, p. 73.
12. Matthew 9:2, in both the New English Bible and the New International Version.
13. Colledge & Walsh, *Julian of Norwich. Showings*, p. 320, Seventy-second Chapter (Long text).
14. ibid. p. 153, Chapter xvii (Short text).
15. Harold S. Kushner, *When Bad Things Happen to Good People*, p. 91.
16. *Janet Scott, *What Canst Thou Say?*, Swarthmore Lecture (Quaker Home Service 1980).
17. 'Spirituality in Counselling: A View from the Other Side' in the *British Journal of Guidance and Counselling*, Vol 18, No 3 (September 1990).
18. Carl Gustav Jung, 'The Relations between the Ego and the Unconscious' in *Two Essays on Analytical Psychology*, p. 219.
19. Christopher Bryant, *The Heart in Pilgrimage*, p. 33.
20. 'The Hymn of Jesus' from the apocryphal *Acts of John*, quoted by *Victor Gollancz in *From Darkness to Light*, p. 176. The Greek and

NOTES

English texts are in Dr M. R. James, *Apocrypha Anecdota* Series 2 (Cambridge 1897), pp. 1–25; and G. R. S. Mead apparently discussed it fully in *Echoes from Gnosis: The Dance of Jesus* (1896), which I have not been able to obtain. This beautiful poem is possibly behind the fifteenth-century 'Tomorrow shall be my dancing day', which we now know in a modern form as 'The Lord of the Dance'.

21. *Harry Williams, *Becoming What I Am* (Darton, Longman & Todd), p. 75.
22. *Paul Tillich, *The Courage to Be* (Fontana 1952).
23. Paul Tillich, *Morality and Beyond*, p. 20.
24. ibid. p. 26.
25. Alan Jones, *Soul Making*, p. 118.
26. Matthew Fox, *Original Blessing*, p. 85.
27. Timothy Ware, *The Orthodox Church*, p. 226. The quotation is Psalm 81:6 from the Orthodox translation, Psalm 82:6 in the Authorized Version.
28. The term is from Thomas Aquinas, XI *De Malo*, 3 & 4.

## 7: Letting Go and Losing

1. *Anthony Bloom, *Living Prayer* (Darton, Longman & Todd, Libra Books 1966), p. 12.
2. London Yearly Meeting of the Religious Society of Friends, Epistle, 1988.
3. Christopher Bryant, *The Heart in Pilgrimage*, p. 55 (my italics).
4. John 12:24, Authorized Version.
5. Christopher Bryant, *The Heart in Pilgrimage*, p. 62.
6. Mary Shideler, *The Theology of Romantic Love*, p. 159.
7. Dag Hammarskjöld, *Markings*, p. 70.
8. John 8:32, Authorized Version.
9. John Sanford, *The Man Who Wrestled with God*, pp. 17 & 20.
10. *Gabriel Marcel, *Homo Viator: introduction to a metaphysic of hope* (Gollancz 1942), pp. 50–2.
11. ibid. pp. 62–3.
12. Isaiah 43:18–19, New International Version.
13. 'Thy faith hath saved thee. Go in peace.' (Luke 7:50, Authorized Version).
14. Matthew Fox, *Original Blessing*, p. 164.
15. *Teilhard de Chardin, *Le Milieu Divin* (Fontana 1964), p. 88.
16. Matthew Fox, *Original Blessing*, p. 164.
17. Gerald Vann, in the introduction to *Gustav Thibon's *Love and Marriage* (Burns & Oates 1962).
18. John Sanford, *The Man Who Wrestled with God*, p. 79.

## NOTES

19. *Robert Llewelyn, *Enfolded in Love: Daily Readings with Julian of Norwich* (Darton, Longman & Todd 1980), p. 55.
20. Matthew Fox, *Original Blessing*, p. 164.
21. *Desmond Tillyer, *Union with God* (Mowbray 1984), p. 71.
22. ibid. p. 70.
23. ibid. p. 71.
24. Christopher Bryant, *The Heart in Pilgrimage*, p. 48.
25. Paul Tillich, *The Courage to Be*, p. 15.
26. Desmond Tillyer, *Union with God*, p. 75.
27. William Leddra, a Quaker of Barbados, on the day before he was martyred in March 1661 (*Christian Faith and Practice*, Extract 34).
28. Christopher Bryant, *The Heart in Pilgrimage*, p. 54.
29. *A. Poulain SJ, *The Graces of Interior Prayer: A Treatise on Mystical Theology* (Kegan Paul, Trench, Trubner & Co 1928), p. 206.
30. Philippians 2:13–14, Authorized Version.
31. Matthew Fox, *Original Blessing*, p. 141.
32. ibid. p. 142.
33. Poulain, *The Graces of Interior Prayer*, p. 201.
34. Alan Jones, *Soul Making*, p. 170.
35. ibid. p. 170.
36. *Baron von Hügel, *Spiritual Counsels and Letters* (Darton, Longman & Todd 1964), pp. 90–1.
37. *C. S. Lewis, *The Great Divorce* (Geoffrey Bles 1946, Fontana 1971), pp. 62–3.


## 8: There is No Wrath in God

1. Matthew Fox, *Original Blessing*, p. 26.
2. 1 John 4:8, Authorized Version.
3. Quoted in *John Fletcher, *Situation Ethics: The New Morality* (SCM Press 1966).
4. Colledge & Walsh, *Julian of Norwich. Showings*, p. 264, Forty-ninth Chapter (Long text).
5. ibid. p. 257, Forty-fifth Chapter (Long text).
6. ibid. p. 264, Forty-ninth Chapter (Long text).
7. ibid. p. 259, Forty-sixth Chapter (Long text).
8. ibid. p. 262, Forty-eighth Chapter (Long text).
9. Jeremiah 9:24, Authorized Version.
10. Both quoted by *Edwin Muir in *The Story and the Fable: an Autobiography* (Rowantree 1987).
11. Jeremiah 31:33–4.
12. *Charles Williams, *He Came Down from Heaven and The Forgiveness of Sins* (Faber & Faber 1950), p. 40.
13. ibid. p. 129.

14. *Robert Llewelyn & Edward Moss (eds), *Fire from a Flint: Daily Readings with William Law* (Darton, Longman & Todd 1986), p. 8.
15. *John Skinner, *Prophecy and Religion* (CUP 1951), p. 229, quoted by Kazoh Kitamori, *Theology of the Pain of God*, p. 67.
16. Colledge & Walsh, *Julian of Norwich. Showings*, p. 246, Fortieth Chapter (Long text).
17. *James Baldwin, *The Fire Next Time* (Penguin Books 1964), p. 81.
18. *Fire from a Flint*, p. 32.
19. Personal communication.
20. Colledge & Walsh, *Julian of Norwich. Showings*.
21. ibid. p. 266, Fiftieth Chapter (Long text).
22. ibid. p. 336, Eightieth Chapter (Long text).
23. Isaiah 43:25–6, Authorized Version.
24. Charles Williams, *The Forgiveness of Sins*, p. 143.
25. Stephen Hobhouse, *Selected Writings of William Law*, Letter IV, quoted by Charles Williams in *The Forgiveness of Sins*, p. 152.
26. *Kazoh Kitamori, *Theology of the Pain of God* (SCM Press 1966, first published 1946), p. 40.
27. *Matthew Fox, *A Spirituality Named Compassion* (San Francisco, Harper, 1984), p. 101.
28. ibid. p. 101.
29. *Martin Luther King, *Strength to Love* (Augsburg Fortress 1981).
30. Alice Miller, *Banished Knowledge*, pp. 171–5 & 193–4.

## 9: The Pain of God

1. *Gerald Vann, *The Pain of Christ and the Sorrow of God* (Blackfriars Publications 1947).
2. Kazoh Kitamori, *Theology of the Pain of God*, pp. 93–4.
3. An Anglican bishop (unnamed), quoted on the radio.
4. Gerald Vann, *The Pain of Christ and the Sorrow of God*, p. 63.
5. Kazoh Kitamori, *Theology of the Pain of God*, p. 103.
6. ibid. p. 167.
7. ibid. p. 156.
8. ibid. p. 64.
9. ibid. p. 159–60.
10. Jeremiah 31:20, New English Bible.
11. Jeremiah 30:17, and 31:3, 9 & 13, New English Bible.
12. Jeremiah 31:21, 22 & 23, New English Bible.
13. Jeremiah 31:34, New English Bible.
14. M. Scott Peck, *People of the Lie*, p. 204.
15. Kazoh Kitamori, *Theology of the Pain of God*, p. 52.
16. ibid. p. 91.
17. ibid. p. 91.

# NOTES

18. ibid. p. 52.
19. Matthew Fox, *Original Blessing*, p. 184.
20. *Charles Williams, 'The Way of Exchange', *Selected Writings* (Oxford University Press 1961), p. 129.
21. Mary Shideler, *The Theology of Romantic Love*, p. 157; quoting *Charles Williams, *The Descent of the Dove: A Short History of the Holy Spirit in the Church* (Faber & Faber 1950), p. 30.
22. ibid. p. 158.
23. ibid. p. 158.
24. Charles Williams, *He Came Down from Heaven*, p. 25.
25. Mary Shideler, *The Theology of Romantic Love*, p. 155.
26. ibid. p. 160.
27. Galatians 6:2.
28. Mary Shideler, *The Theology of Romantic Love*, p. 151.
29. Genesis 9:5, Authorized Version.
30. Grace Jantzen, *Julian of Norwich*, p. 171.
31. Matthew Fox, *Original Blessing*, p. 44.
32. Kenji Miyazawa, quoted in Matthew Fox, *Original Blessing*, p. 142.
33. Matthew Fox, *Original Blessing*, pp. 144, 145 & 147.
34. *Carl Gustav Jung, *Psychological Types, or The Psychology of Individuation*, p. 605 (Routledge & Kegan Paul 1964).
35. Kazoh Kitamori, *Theology of the Pain of God*, p. 62.
36. ibid. p. 62.
37. Teilhard de Chardin, *Le Milieu Divin*, p. 88.
38. Kazoh Kitamori, *Theology of the Pain of God*, p. 156.
39. Matthew Fox, *Original Blessing*, p. 119.
40. ibid. p. 218.
41. Teilhard de Chardin, *Human Energy*, p. 49 (my italics).
42. Gerald Vann, *The Pain of Christ and the Sorrow of God*, pp. 50 and 75.

## Epilogue: Traveller's Harvest

1. Charles Williams, *He Came Down from Heaven*, p. 93.
2. ibid. p. 92.
3. Meister Eckhart, quoted by Matthew Fox, *Original Blessing*, p. 265.
4. Teilhard de Chardin, *Le Milieu Divin*, pp. 71–2.
5. ibid. pp. 60–1.
6. *A. N. Whitehead, *Adventures of Ideas* (Collier-Macmillan 1967), p. 286.